G000069148

Available in the same series

Amsterdam
Athens
Berlin
Brussels
Copenhagen
Florence
Frankfurt
Hamburg
Hong Kong
Jerusalem
London
Madrid
Munich
New York
Paris
Rome
San Francisco
Singapore
Tokyo
Venice
Vienna

Baedeker's

AA

Frankfurt

THE AUTOMOBILE ASSOCIATION

Imprint

Cover picture: Römer, with Bank für Gemeinwirtschaft to rear

71 colour photographs
13 ground plans, 4 special plans, 2 perspective drawings, 1 transport plan, 1 city plan

Conception and editorial work:
Redaktionsbüro Harenberg, Schwerte

English Language: Alec Court

Text:
Heike Risse, Ingrid Rödel, Volker Rödel

General direction:
Dr Peter Baumgarten, Baedeker Stuttgart

Cartography:
Ingenieurbüro für kartographie Huber & Oberländer, Munich
Mairs Geographischer Verlag GmbH & Co., Ostfildern-Kemnat (city plan)

English translation:
James Hogarth

Source of illustrations:
Alte Oper (1), Amt für Fremdenverkehr (1), Historia-Photo (3), Sperber (65), ZEFA (1)

Following the tradition established by Karl Baedeker in 1844, sights of particular interest and hotels of particular quality are distinguished by either one or two asterisks.

To make it easier to locate the various sights listed in the "A to Z" section of the Guide, their coordinates on the large city plan (and on the smaller inset plan of the city centre) are shown in red at the head of each entry.

Only a selection of hotels and restaurants can be given: no reflection is implied, therefore, on establishments not included.

In a time of rapid change it is difficult to ensure that all the information given is entirely accurate and up to date, and the possibility of error can never be entirely eliminated. Although the publishers can accept no responsibility for inaccuracies and omissions, they are always grateful for corrections and suggestions for improvement.

1st edition

© 1983 Baedeker Stuttgart
Original German edition

© 1985 Jarrold and Sons Ltd
English language edition worldwide

© 1985 The Automobile Association 57163
United Kingdom and Ireland

Licensed user:
Mairs Geographischer Verlag GmbH & Co., Ostfildern-Kemnat bei Stuttgart

Reproductions:
Gölz Repro-Service GmbH, Ludwigsburg

The name *Baedeker* is a registered trademark

Printed in Great Britain by Jarrold and Sons Ltd, Norwich

ISBN 0 86145 322 0

Contents

	Page
The Principal Sights at a Glance	inside front cover
Preface	7
Facts and Figures	9
General	9
Population and Religion	11
Transport	11
Culture	12
Commerce and Industry	13
Notable Personalities	15
History of Frankfurt	19
Sights from A to Z	30
Practical Information	130
Useful Telephone Numbers	171
Transport plan (S- and U-Bahn)	inside back cover
City plan	at end of book

Preface

This Pocket Guide to Frankfurt is one of the new generation of Baedeker guides.

Baedeker pocket guides, illustrated throughout in colour, are designed to meet the needs of the modern traveller. They are quick and easy to consult, with the principal features of interest described in alphabetical order and practical details about location, opening times, etc., shown in the margin.

Each city guide is divided into three parts. The first part gives a general account of the city, its history, notable personalities and so on; in the second part the principal sights are described; and the third part contains a variety of practical information designed to help visitors to find their way about and make the most of their stay.

The Baedeker pocket guides are noted for their concentration on essentials and their convenience of use. They contain numerous specially drawn plans and coloured illustrations, and in a pocket at the back of the book is a large plan of the city. Each entry in the main part of the guide gives the coordinates of the square on the plan in which the particular feature can be located. Users of this guide, therefore, will have no difficulty in finding what they want to see.

Facts and Figures

Frankfurt's
coat of arms

General

Frankfurt am Main – to be distinguished from Frankfurt an der Oder, in East Germany – is a major commercial and industrial centre and the largest city in the *Land* (district) of Hessen.
The city's coat of arms displays a silver eagle with outspread wings, wearing the municipal crown, on a red ground; its heraldic colours are white and red.

Geographical situation

Frankfurt's tallest historical monument, the spire of the Cathedral, which serves as a triangulation point, is located in latitude 50°6'42.5" N and longitude 8°41'22.4" E. The base of the tower lies 100 m (328 ft) above sea-level. The highest point within the city is the hill (212 m (696 ft)) to the east on which the Berger Warte stands; its lowest point (88 m (289 ft)) is on the Main where it leaves the city area at Sindlingen, in the west. Frankfurt lies on both banks of the Main, some 36 km (22 miles) above its junction with the Rhine, in the fertile region between the Spessart and Taunus hills. The river's wide flood plain narrows due to the hills which are only some 400 m (440 yd) apart at this point and this made for an easier river crossing and formed an important link between north and south. This was the starting-point of the settlement which became Frankfurt.
The city is bounded on the north by the little River Nidda and on the south by the Stadtwald (Town Forest).

Climate

The climate of Frankfurt is conditioned by the Taunus hills which shelter it on the north-west and north and by its situation in the low-lying Main plain. The combination of these factors gives it a winter which is normally mild, an early spring and a long autumn. The relative frequency of windless days and the building-up of open spaces tend to restrict the circulation of air within the city area, and industrial, traffic and domestic emissions may lead, particularly in winter, to the development of smog.

Area and population

The city has an area of 249 sq. km (96 sq. miles), with a maximum extent of 23.3 km (14½ miles) from north to south and about the same from east to west. The city boundaries have a total length of some 113 km (70 miles). The total area includes 8415 ha (20,875 acres) of pasture and arable land and gardens, 4248 ha (10,493 acres) of woodland and forest, 529 ha (1307 acres) of lakes, rivers, canals and streams, 5641 ha (13,933 acres) of built-up area, 3519 ha (8692 acres) of public streets and squares, and 2535 ha (6261 acres) devoted to other purposes.
Frankfurt's population shows a slight falling trend, from 631,234 in 1979 to 626,941 in 1981; the latter figure includes 138,352 foreigners.

◀ *The Römer, Frankfurt's historic old Town Hall*

Facts and Figures

The skyline of "Mainhattan"

Administration

The citizens of Frankfurt elect the 93 members of the municipal parliament, who in turn elect the Magistrat (municipal authority), the political heads of the administration.

The Magistrat consists of the Chief Burgomaster, the Burgomaster (who acts as his deputy), the City Chamberlain, eight full-time members and twelve honorary members.

The full-time members of the Magistrat, each responsible for a particular department of the administration, are appointed for a six-year term, irrespective of the sessions of the municipal parliament. This ensures a certain continuity of administration.

City wards

The city is divided into 46 wards, which for the most part follow the boundaries of its former suburbs and outlying districts. Before 1877 the city consisted of the Altstadt (Old Town), Innenstadt (Central Area), Bahnhofsviertel (Station Ward), Gutleutviertel (Gutleut Ward), Gallusviertel (Gallus Ward), Westend, Nordend (North End), Ostend (East End) and Sachsenhausen.

Other communes were later incorporated in the city: Bornheim (1877); Bockenheim (1895); Niederrad, Oberrad and Seckbach (1900); Berkersheim, Bonames, Eckenheim, Eschersheim, Ginnheim, Hausen, Heddernheim, Niederursel, Praunheim, Preungesheim and Rödelheim (1910); Höchst, Sindlingen, Zeilsheim, Unterliederbach, Sossenheim, Nied, Griesheim, Schwanheim and Fechenheim (1928); Kalbach, Nieder-Eschbach, Nieder-Erlenbach and Harheim (1972); and finally Bergen-Enkheim (1977).

Motorway crossing at Frankfurt

Population and Religion

The present population of Frankfurt is some 621,000, including 136,500 foreigners.
The approximate numbers of Roman Catholics and Protestants are: 265,000 Catholics in 56 parishes and 234,000 Protestants in 80 parishes. There are just under 5000 Jews.

Transport

Frankfurt's local transport systems are combined and co-ordinated in the network known as FVV (Frankfurter Verkehrs- und Tarifverbund). Between Mainz/Wiesbaden in the west, Hanau in the east, Friedberg in the north and Darmstadt in the south the same tickets are valid for the S-Bahnen (Stadt-bahnen, City Lines) and buses operated by German Federal Railways and the municipal trams, buses and underground system (U-Bahn) run by the city (Stadtwerke Frankfurt am Main).

Local transport

The city's Central Station, like its airport, is a traffic centre of international importance, with some 1500 trains carrying 250,000 passengers during the working week.

Railways

Frankfurt is served by many motorways and main roads (federal highways).

Trunk roads

11

Culture

Motorways	The A 5 motorway (E 4, the European highway from Puttgarden on the Baltic coast to Basle in Switzerland) to the west of the city and the A 3 (E 5, from Emmerich on the Dutch frontier to Passau on the Austrian frontier) to the south cross one another at the Frankfurter Kreuz (Frankfurt Cross). The A 66 (Fulda–Wiesbaden) runs to the north of the city, the A 661 to the east.
Federal highways	The following federal highways (Bundesstrassen) traverse Frankfurt: B 3 (Hamburg–Basle) B 8 (Düsseldorf–Regensburg) B 40 (Saarbrücken–Fulda) B 43 (Mainz–Hanau) B 44 (Mannheim–Frankfurt).
Airport	In terms of annual throughput of passengers Frankfurt's airport (the Rhine-Main Airport) is second in Europe only to London Heathrow, with 17·7 million passengers a year. In terms of freight traffic it takes first place. In addition to some 4800 arrivals and departures every week by planes belonging to more than 70 airlines, the airport is used by more than 200 charter companies every year. The airport is conveniently situated to the south-west of the city at the Frankfurter Kreuz. The journey to the city centre takes only some 10–15 minutes by S-Bahn (lines S 14 and S 15).

Culture

Higher education	In addition to the University (26,500 students) there are various technical colleges (4500 students), the College of Music (Hochschule für Musik, 600 students) and the State College of Art (Staatliche Hochschule für bildende Künste) or Städelschule (140 students). The courses run by the Adult Education Centre (Volkshochschule) are attended by more than 50,000 students. In Seckbach is the College of the German Book Trade (Schule des Deutschen Buchhandels), a vocational training centre for the German publishing and bookselling trade.
Museums	Of Frankfurt's 15 museums the Städel Museum, the Liebieghaus and the Senckenberg Museum of Natural History are of more than regional importance. In addition the city has seven archive and record offices.
Theatres	Frankfurt has five theatres which put on more than 200 performances a year, as well as 12 cabaret theatres and theatres without a regular programme.
Concerts	Concerts are given by the Frankfurter Museumsgesellschaft (Frankfurt Museum Society: Opera House Orchestra and Museum Orchestra), the Hessischer Rundfunk (Hessen Radio Corporation: Hessen Radio Symphony Orchestra), the Frankfurter Kunstgemeinde (Frankfurt Art Union), the Vereinigung für Musikpflege (Association for the Advancement of Music) and various Church and other concert organisations. The Old Opera House has a concert hall (opened in August 1981) with excellent acoustics and seating for an audience of some 2400.

Johann Wolfgang Goethe University

Commerce and Industry

Sales tax statistics show that Frankfurt has an annual turnover subject to tax of well over 100 billion DM. Just under half of this total is accounted for by industry (more than 600 firms), followed by wholesale trade (some 2400 firms), retail trade (over 4000 firms) and some 3800 small workshops.

General

Starting from the early annual fairs of the medieval period, Frankfurt has developed into a European commercial centre and an international financial and exchange market. In 1585, seeking to obviate the uncertainties of currency transactions the merchants of Frankfurt set up an organisation to establish binding rates of exchange – the origin of the present Stock Exchange. The city now also has a Currency Exchange, a Real Estate Exchange, a Corn and Produce Exchange and a Gold Exchange.

Commerce

The figures of commercial turnover – 32·9 billion DM for wholesale and retail trade – point to the importance of commerce in the city's economy. Of central importance are wholesaling and foreign trade, in a variety of fields – foodstuffs, cereals, feed products and fertilisers, motor vehicles and machinery, pharmaceuticals, textiles, leather goods, tobacco wares and furs. The Central Market is one of the largest centres of the fruit and vegetable trade in the Federal Republic.

Frankfurt's retail trade, concentrated in the pedestrian precincts of the city centre – the Zeil, Schillerstrasse, Grosse Bockenheimer Strasse (popularly known as the Fressgass, "Guzzling Street"), Kaiserstrasse – has made a major contribution to the

13

city's ranking as one of the great commercial centres of the Federal Republic.

Trade fairs

As a centre for trade fairs and exhibitions, and consequently in the associated fields of advertising and publicity, Frankfurt occupies a leading place in West Germany. Regular events are:
IMA – International Vending and Entertainment Machines Fair
Heimtextil – International Domestic Textiles Fair
Frankfurt International Fair (spring and autumn)
IAA – International Motor Show (every other year, alternating with International Fur Show)
Interstoff – Clothing Textiles Show (spring and autumn)
ACHEMA – Chemical Industries Fair
Frankfurt Book Fair.

Trade associations

Frankfurt is the headquarters of many trade associations and federations. In addition to some 40 regional and provincial associations there are national organisations concerned with tourism, transport, the tobacco and fur industries, the book trade, agriculture, engineering and the automobile industry.

Banks

Frankfurt is the undisputed financial centre of the German Federal Republic. From the currency dealings associated with the town's trade fairs there arose in the 16th and 17th c. a number of banking houses, some of which still exist as private banks. Then during the 19th c. the financing of international railway lines, wars and other government activities gave the city a disproportionately high number of banks (in 1850 one for every 170 inhabitants). After the establishment of the German Empire in 1871 the centre of banking activity in Germany moved to Berlin, but it returned to Frankfurt after the Second World War, partly as a result of the foundation there of the Bank of the German Länder, predecessor of the present German Federal Bank.
In the city's banking quarter, concentrated round the Taunus Gardens, there are now the offices of 346 credit institutions, including the "big three' German banks (Deutsche Bank, Dresdner Bank, Commerzbank) and 196 foreign banks, with 120 agencies and 76 subsidiaries and branches. They include both public, private and co-operative institutions. Some 75 per cent of the world's leading credit institutions, as well as financial agencies of the Comecon countries (Soviet Union, Romania, Poland), have branches in Frankfurt.

Industry

Frankfurt became involved in the general industrial development of Germany only at a very late stage. It was not until the proclamation of freedom of trade on 1 May 1864 that the establishment of factories in the city became an attractive proposition for industrialists. Since there were no resources of raw materials in the area it was mainly the processing industries that developed in Frankfurt, earning an international reputation by product specialisation and high quality.
The most important Frankfurt industries are mechanical and electrical engineering and chemicals, but there are also efficient and productive firms in the building and construction industries, printing and publishing and the manufacture of foodstuffs.

German Federal Bank

Notable Personalities

Bettina, sister of Clemens Brentano (see entry), was born in Frankfurt, and in 1811 married Achim von Arnim, one of the leading representatives of the later Romantic school. She herself wrote novels in the form of letters, based on an imaginative reworking of her correspondence with Goethe, Karoline von Günderode and her brother, all of whom she enthusiastically admired: "Goethe's Correspondence with a Child" (1835), "Die Günderode" (1840), "Clemens Brentano's Spring Garland" (1844).

Bettina von Arnim-Brentano (1785–1859)

Simon Moritz von Bethmann inherited a family banking house (founded 1748), which under his direction achieved international prominnce. As a high official and diplomat in the Russian service he was able to persuade Napoleon not to march his troops through Frankfurt in 1813. He also showed himself a generous patron of the city's cultural life. There is a monument to him behind the Ariadneum (Odeon) in the Friedberg Gardens, which he founded. His uncle, with the same name (1721–82), was a patron of the Bürgerhospital.

Simon Moritz von Bethmann (1786–1826)

The poet Clemens Brentano, brother of Bettina von Arnim (see entry), was born in Ehrenbreitstein on the Rhine and spent his childhood in the house Zum goldenen Kopf in the old Grosse Sandgasse (now part of the Berliner Strasse) in Frankfurt. His works include a famous collection of German folk-songs, "Des Knaben Wunderhorn" (1805–08).

Clemens Brentano (1778–1842)

Notable Personalities

Paul Johann Anselm, Ritter von Feuerbach (1775–1833)

Born at Hainichen, near Jena, the jurist Anselm von Feuerbach acquired the foundations of his classical culture at the Gymnasium Francofortanum, a grammar school in Frankfurt. Later, as professor at Jena, Kiel and Landshut, he became the founder of the modern German school of criminal law. His works included the Bavarian Penal Code of 1813 and studies of the psychology of criminals. He is buried in the Main Cemetery in Frankfurt.

Erich Fromm (1900–80)

The psychoanalyst Erich Fromm, one of the leading neo-Freudians, was born in Frankfurt but emigrated in 1934 to the United States, where he lectured at various universities and finally became Professor of Psychiatry at New York University. His most important works are "Escape from Freedom", "Man for Himself", "Psychoanalysis and Religion", "The Dogma of Christ" and "The Sane Society".

Johann Wolfgang von Goethe (1749–1832)

The son of an Imperial official, Johann Kaspar Goethe (1710–82), and Elisabeth Catharina Textor (1731–1808), Goethe spent his early years in Frankfurt – a period described in his autobiography, "Dichtung und Wahrheit". The house in which he was born is in the Grosser Hirschgraben. Here he began the first version of "Faust" and wrote, in addition to numerous poems, his plays "Götz von Berlichingen" and "Clavigo" (1773) and his novel "Werther" (1774). In 1775 he left Frankfurt for Weimar.

Goethe is commemorated by a monument in the Gallus Gardens. His father's grave is in the Petersfriedhof, and his mother is buried in the Textor family tomb surrounded by a semi circular colonnade in the courtyard of the Liebfrauenschule.

In 1927 the city of Frankfurt founded the Goethe Prize, to be awarded to men and women worthy of an honour associated with the name of Goethe. A list of recipients of the Goethe Prize is on p. 29.

Johannes Gensfleisch, known as Gutenberg (c. 1397–1468)

The inventor of printing with movable type lived in Frankfurt from 1454 to 1457, after giving up his workshop in Mainz to his creditors Hans Fust and Fust's son-in-law Peter Schöffer. Here he printed some letters of indulgence, the "Türkenkalender" and Pope Calixtus III's Bull calling for a Crusade against the Turks. He died in Mainz in 1468.

In the Rossmarkt is a monument to Gutenberg (by Eduard Schmidt von der Launitz, 1858). It depicts Gutenberg with Fust and Schöffer, accompanied by allegorical figures.

Otto Hahn (1879–1968)

The chemist Otto Hahn, born in Frankfurt, became Director of the Emperor William Institute of Chemistry in Berlin in 1928, and in 1938, together with Friedrich Strassmann, discovered the process of nuclear fission of the atoms of uranium and thorium, for which he and Strassmann were awarded the 1944 Nobel Prize for chemistry. From 1948 to 1959 he was President of the Max Planck Society. In 1959 he was made an honorary citizen of Frankfurt, and in 1969 the city established the Otto Hahn Foundation.

Friedrich Hölderlin (1770–1843)

The poetry of Friedrich Hölderlin was long in securing recognition, and it was only after the First World War that the quality of his work, particularly his lyric poetry, was properly appreciated. From 1796 to 1798 he was tutor in the household of a Frankfurt banker, J. F. Gontard, and fell in love with

Goethe

Hölderlin

Schopenhauer

Gontard's wife Susette, whom he celebrated in his poems under the name of Diotima. Under this inspiration his years in Frankfurt were a poetically fertile period. His later years were disturbed and unhappy, blighted by mental derangement. Much of his novel in letter form, "Hyperion", was written in Frankfurt, as was his unfinished drama "The Death of Empedocles".

Hamman was perhaps the most prominent representative of one of Frankfurt's oldest patrician families, which for centuries supplied councillors and burgomasters for the running of the city's affairs. During the Reformation period he was the leading figure in the municipal council. He owned the Holzhausen-schlösschen, his family's country residence, then a medieval moated castle, which in 1722–28 was rebuilt in Baroque style by the French architect Rémy de la Fosse and now houses the Museum of Prehistory.
The Municipal Archives contain the Holzhausen family records, one of the largest collections of records of a patrician family, going back to the 13th c.

Hamman von Holzhausen (1467–1536)

The composer Paul Hindemith, a native of Hanau, studied under Arnold Mendelssohn and Bernhard Sekles at Dr Koch's Conservatoire and from 1915 to 1927 was Musical Director of the Frankfurt Opera House. Thereafter, until leaving Germany in 1933, he was a professor at the College of Music in Berlin. From 1940 to 1953 he taught at Yale University, and thereafter at the University of Zürich. While living in the Kuhhirtenturm in Frankfurt he composed his opera "Cardillac" and parts of "Mathis der Maler".

Paul Hindemith (1895–1963)

Heinrich Hoffmann was a doctor as well as a writer. In 1834 he founded a hospice for the destitute, and from 1851 to 1889 was Director of the Frankfurt municipal institution for epileptics and the insane, on a site now occupied by the I.G. Farben office building. He is much more widely known, however, as author of the children's book "Struwwelpeter", written in 1844. He died in Frankfurt in 1894.

Heinrich Hoffmann (1809–94)

Ernst May played a decisive part in the development of housing and town planning in Germany. As Frankfurt's Municipal Architect from 1925 to 1930 he evolved a new approach to

Ernst May (1886–1970)

housing. On the basis of a development plan prepared by him there came into being within a relatively short space of time a ring of new housing developments on the outskirts of Frankfurt, including the well-known Römerstadt estate (1927–28), the Bornheimer Hang scheme (1926–29) and the Höhenblick development at Ginnheim (1926–27). His ten-year house-building programme, designed to relieve the city's acute housing shortage, was considerably exceeded in the first five years. It was not so much the scale of his activities, however, that made Frankfurt the starting-point of modern housing development, but rather his revolutionary approach to the planning and design of his housing schemes.

In 1930 May went to Moscow. He became responsible for the planning of Magnitogorsk, Stalinsk and other industrial towns and produced a development plan for Moscow based on a system of satellite towns.

Thereafter he spent three years in Tanganyika as a farmer before setting up as an architect in Nairobi in 1937. In 1954 he became head of the planning department of a large firm of house-builders in Hamburg, and later was in private practice as an architect and planner.

Matthäus Merian the Elder
(1593–1650)

Merian, a painter and engraver, was born in Basle. In 1624 he went to Frankfurt, were he acquired the rights of citizenship by marrying into a family of art publishers. There he produced a long series of views of German and European towns, published in Frankfurt between 1624 and 1688 in his "Topographia". He died in 1650 while taking the cure at Schwalbach. He is commemorated by a statue in the courtyard of the Town Hall.

Meyer Amschel Rothschild
(1743–1812)

Meyer Amschel Rothschild was the founder of the Rothschild banking house in Frankfurt, which brought his five sons international fame. The firm had branches in Paris, London, Vienna and Naples. The headquarters of this famous banking family, which was ennobled by the Austrian Emperor in 1817, were in Börnestrasse (formerly Judengasse) from 1798 to 1901; the building was destroyed in 1944.

The Rothschilds were generous benefactors of Frankfurt. There is a park named after them on the Bockenheimer Landstrasse (corner of Reuterweg).

Arthur Schopenhauer
(1788–1860)

The philosopher Arthur Schopenhauer moved from Berlin to Frankfurt in 1831 to escape a cholera epidemic and lived there as a private scholar. From 1843 until his death he stayed in the street called An der Schönen Aussicht (Nos. 16 and 17). His principal work, "The World as Will and Idea" (two volumes, 1818 and 1859), was the culmination of the German idealist school. The real impact of his work came only in the second half of the 19th c. Among those whom he influenced were Wagner, Wilhelm Raabe, Nietzsche and Freud.

Schopenhauer's library and manuscripts, together with personal mementoes and literature on his philosophy, are preserved in the Schopenhauer Archives in the Municipal and University Library.

Johann Christian
Senckenberg (1707–72)

Senckenberg, a doctor and natural scientist, devoted his fortune in 1763 to the building of the Bürgerhospital and a medical and scientific institute, which were to become the basis of the Johann Wolfgang Goethe University. His library was the foundation of the Senckenberg Library. The Senckenberg Society for the Study of Nature, founded on the initiative of Goethe, established the Senckenberg Natural History Museum in 1821. Senckenberg's grave is at the old entrance to the Bürgerhospital.

The Frankfurt banker Johann Friedrich Städel bequeathed his large art collection together with a million florins for the establishment of an art institute. The picture gallery popularly known merely as "the Städel" now possesses one of the richest collections in Germany, and the Städelschule (State College of Art), also due to Städel's munificence, has departments of graphic art, painting, architecture and sculpture.

Johann Friedrich Städel (1728–1816)

As Prussian Minister from 1804 to 1807 and again in 1808 Stein was responsible for a series of reforms (abolition of serfdom, municipal reorganisation, etc.). Becoming adviser to Tsar Alexander I in 1812, he was instrumental in bringing about the alliance between Prussia and Russia which led to the defeat of Napoleon; and as the Tsar's confidential envoy at the Congress of Vienna he was able to secure the independence of Frankfurt within the German Confederation, for which he was made an honorary citizen in 1816. In 1819 he played an influential part in the foundation of the Early German History Society in Frankfurt. He died in Schloss Cappenberg in Westphalia.

Heinrich Friedrich Karl, Reichsfreiherr vom and zum Stein (1757–1831)

Friedrich Stoltze was Frankfurt's best known and most popular dialect writer. The son of a restaurant proprietor, he was born in the house Zum Rebstock, which about 1830 became a meeting-place of radical democrats; the Custom House was built on the site in 1929. Stoltze was Editor of the "Krebbelzeitung" (from 1852) and the satirical "Frankfurter Latern", after the suspension of which he was compelled to go into exile. There is a Stoltze Museum in Töngesgasse.

Friedrich Stoltze (1816–91)

History of Frankfurt

The hill at the ford over the Main where the Cathedral now stands has been continuously occupied since the Bronze Age.

Bronze Age

After Domitian's victorious campaign against the Chatti the Taunus and Wetterau come under Roman rule. To protect the frontier a *limes* is laid out from the junction of the Kinzig with the Main to the Vinxtbach, defended by numerous forts. The principal fort is at Heddernheim on the north bank of the Nidda, corresponding approximately to the area of the old town within the Staufen walls. There seems also to have been a fort on the Cathedral hill.

A.D. 83/84

Trajan abandons the forts in the Wetterau plain (the Civitas Tavnensium) and moves Roman forces forward to the limes. The Heddernheim fort develops into the little town of Nida.

About 110

The Alemanni overrun the Upper German limes; almost the whole of the territory on the right bank of the Rhine is lost to the Romans. Nida, now surrounded by a wall, is destroyed and lies desolate until the late medieval period (now the Römerstadt and Nordweststadt districts).
An Alemannic settlement is established on the Cathedral hill, later to develop into the Frankish Villa Regia ("royal town").

About 260

History of Frankfurt

About 500   The Franks, led by Chlodwig (Clovis), expel the Alemanni and make the territories on the Main and Middle Rhine their heartland.

About 700   The Frankish royal stronghold on the Cathedral hill is rebuilt in stone.

794   First documentary reference to the Frankish royal stronghold on the Cathedral hill as Villa Franconovurd ("ford of the Franks"). At an Imperial Synod held here Charlemagne rejects the decisions of the Council of Nicaea (787) and asserts his independence of Byzantium. The royal palace, also first referred to in connection with the Synod, becomes the favourite residence of the East Frankish kings.

804   Final subjugation of the Saxons by Charlemagne. The name of the Frankfurt district of Sachsenhausen may reflect a forcible resettlement of Saxons in Franconia (though the name does not appear in the records until 1193).

About 852   King Ludwig (Louis) the German builds a church dedicated to the Saviour (St Salvator) and a foundation for secular clergy – forerunners of the later Cathedral of St Bartholomew and its associated collegiate foundation.

856   First installation of a king in Frankfurt: Lothar II receives the kingdom of Lorraine (the territory between the North Sea and the sources of the Maas/Meuse and Moselle).

887   First election of a king in Frankfurt: after the deposition of the Emperor Charles III Arnulf of Carinthia is chosen as King of the Eastern Franks.

941   Reconciliation between King Otto I and his rebellious brother Henry, who makes his submission, in the garb of a penitent, in the royal palace at Frankfurt.

1074   The Emperor Henry IV grants the citizens of Worms freedom from customs duties in Frankfurt – an indication of the increasing importance of Frankfurt as a commercial centre.

1138   Election of Conrad III, the first king of the Staufen dynasty. Between 1140 and his death in 1152 Conrad stays in Frankfurt on eight occasions (1140, 1141, 1142, 1146, twice in 1147, 1149, 1152). During this period work begins on the construction of the Staufen palace, with the Saalhof. The town is surrounded by walls (the "Staufen walls").

1142   Princely Diet held in Frankfurt: reconciliation between the Staufens and the Guelphs. – Frankfurt is now increasingly favoured as the meeting-place of Synods, Imperial Diets, etc.

1147   Imperial Diet in Frankfurt. King Conrad III, influenced by the preaching of Bernard of Clairvaux (on 27 December 1146 in Speyer), resoles to go on Crusade; he declares a general peace within the Empire and has his ten-year-old son Henry (d. 1150) elected King.

1152   Conrad III dies in Frankfurt. His nephew Frederick I Barbarossa is elected king in Frankfurt. Thereafter he stays in Frankfurt on six occasions (1158, 1163, twice in 1166, 1170, 1173) and enlarges the royal palace.

Completion of the Saalhof (Aula Regia).   1170–75

The royal steward, the highest official in the royal palace, gives   About 1200
place to a mayor, who becomes responsible, together with a
college of jurors, for the royal court of justice and the
administration of the town: the first step towards a municipal
council.

Otto IV, a Guelph, is unanimously elected king, and the   1208
Staufens are compelled to hand over the royal insignia to the
Guelphs. To provide for their safe-keeping Otto builds a
temporary chapel adjoining the Saalhof (which still exists).

Frederick II presents the hospital in Sachsenhausen to the   1221
Teutonic Order.

First mention in the records of wooden bridge over the Main.   1222

Building of the Cathedral (St Bartholomew) on the site of the   1238–39
earlier Church of St Salvator (852).

First mention of the Frankfurt Fair, to which the Emperor   1240
Frederick II gives his patronage.

Frankfurt joins the League of Rhenish Towns, established to   1254
preserve peace and maintain the towns' municipal and
economic interests during an imperial interregnum; by 1256 it
consists of over 70 towns as well as a number of secular and
ecclesiastical princedoms. In 1255 King William of Holland
takes over the leadership of the League.

First reference to the Frankfurt municipal council, consisting   1266
not only of the mayor and jurors but also representatives of the
townspeople ("second bench") and, from about 1320,
craftsmen ("third bench").

End of the interregnum: Count Rudolf of Habsburg is elected   1273
king in Frankfurt.

Frankfurt, Friedberg, Wetzlar and Gelnhausen form the   1285
Wetterau League of Towns.

First reference to a municipal charter.   1297

Double election of Ludwig the Bavarian (a Wittelsbach) and   1314
Frederick the Handsome (a Habsburg). Ludwig pays particular
attention to Frankfurt.

Emperor Ludwig the Bavarian authorises Frankfurt to hold a   1330
second annual fair during Lent. With this spring fair the town
achieves international importance.

Ludwig agrees to the extension of the town to more than twice   1333
its previous area.

Imperial Diet in Frankfurt. The Imperial Electors, with the   1339
exception of the Archbishop of Cologne, assert their view that

the king whom they elect does not require to be approved by the Pope.

From 1343	A new wall is built round the town.
1349	Outbreak of plague in Frankfurt.
1356	The Emperor Charles IV, in the Golden Bull (an Imperial Edict regulating the royal election procedure and the rights of the Electors), lays down that the election is to take place in Frankfurt. The election is held in the Church of St Bartholomew, which has the status of an Imperial Cathedral.
1366	The Frankfurt patricians, under the leadership of Mayor Siegfried zum Paradies, repress unrest among members of the guilds. Siegried zum Paradies redeems the office of mayor, which had been pledged for security, along with other pledges.
1372	The Frankfurt municipal council acquires the pledges redeemed by Siegfried zum Paradies. Having gained ownership of the office of mayor, Frankfurt becomes a free city of the Empire.
1381	After an attack by a league of knights Frankfurt joins with Mainz, Worms, Speyer, Strasbourg, Pfeddersheim and other Imperial free cities in the League of Rhenish Towns, which in the same year concludes a pact of mutual assistance with the Swabian League.
1388	Frankfurt takes part in the war between the towns and the territorial lords, now seeking to increase their power.
1389	Battle of Kronberg. The men of Frankfurt suffer an annihilating defeat at the hands of Count Palatine Ruprecht I and his allies, the Knights of the Taunus, but the town is able to purchase its freedom.
1393	King Wenceslas authorises the construction of an outer circuit of defences, which is begun in 1396.
About 1400	A Frankfurt priest writes a theological and mystical work, published by Luther under the title "A German Theology", which seeks to show "what Adam and Christ are, and how Adam is to die in us and Christ to arise". Some 200 editions of this work are known, including Chinese, Japanese, Russian, Swedish and Danish versions.
1405	Frankfurt acquires the house known as the Römer and adapts it to serve as Town Hall (1405–13).
1415	Construction of the Pfarrturm (Parish Tower), a Frankfurt landmark.
About 1440	Frankfurt has some 9000 inhabitants. The gardeners alone account for 39 families (roughly a third of the population).
1454	Johannes Gutenburg, the inventor of printing with movable metal type, works in Frankfurt.
1462	A ghetto is established for the Jews.

Building of the Stone House.   .   1464

Construction of the Friedberger Warte (watch-tower) to reinforce the town's outer defences. Earlier towers were the Galluswarte (1414), Bockenheimer Warte (1434–35) and Sachsenhäuser Warte (1470–71).   1478

Johannes Kremer, a clerk of court, writes down the text of the Frankfurt Passion Play. The play, which has 4408 lines and lasts three days, is one of the finest German religious plays. The performance of 1498 lasted four days and had a cast of 280. The last recorded performance was in 1506. In 1515 all plays were banned in Frankfurt.   1493

Establishment of the Imperial Supreme Court (Reichskammer-gericht) in Frankfurt.   1495

The Emperor Maximilian increases the privileges of the three Leipzig fairs, which give rise to increasing competition with Frankfurt.   1497

The Frankfurt municipal charter is "reformed" (i.e. adapted to Roman law).   1509

Martin Luther passes through Frankfurt on his way to the Diet of Worms.   1521

The movement of rebellion in towns (which is independent of the peasant wars of the time) reaches Frankfurt: 60 citizens present to the municipal council 42 articles of complaint (selection of parish priests by the council and commune, taxation of the clergy, election of a second burgomaster from the commune, etc.), which are at first accepted but later rejected.   1525

Christian Egenolff establishes the first printing-house of any size in Frankfurt.   1530

Frankfurt formally adopts the Lutheran faith. The Cathedral remains Catholic.   1535

Frankfurt joins the League of Schmalkalden.   1536

The Emperor Charles V extends the provisions of the Nuremberg religious peace (1532) to those estates of the Empire that had adopted the Augsburg Confession, and in return receives assistance in his war with the Turks.   1539

Dissolution of the League of Schmalkalden after the defeat of its forces. Frankfurt is occupied by Imperial troops under Count von Büren.   1546

Dutch and Walloon Protestants, led by the French theologian Valérand Poullain, settle in Frankfurt.   1554

Maximilian II is crowned king in Frankfurt, which now becomes the regular place of coronation.   1562

The book catalogues of the Frankfurt fairs represent the earliest bibliographies of German literature.   1564

History of Frankfurt

1576	Introduction of a regularly levied property tax.
1578	Johann Fichard's important Code of Civil Law comes into force in Frankfurt.
1583	On the occasion of the Frankfurt Fair the first newspaper-type publications appear: the "Fair Relations", containing reports of political and other events.
1585	With the agreement of the municipal council, Italian and Nuremberg merchants establish the Stock Exchange.
1587	The Protestant Frankfurt printer Johann Spiess publishes the "Book of Doctor Faust".
1596	On account of religious tensions with the Lutherans most of the Dutch Protestants leave Frankfurt and settle in Hanau and Frankenthal. About 1600 there are some 2000 Dutch religious refugees in the Frankfurt area, making an important contribution to the economy. Frankfurt also has many Protestants from the Latin countries.
About 1600	Together with Prague, Vienna and Worms, Frankfurt is one of the few Imperial cities with a large Jewish community (some 4500).
1612	The "Fettmilch Rising". Reacting against the arbitrary rule of the patrician municipal council and the Jewish practice of usury, numbers of townspeople, craftsmen and factory workers led by a gingerbread-maker named Vinzenz Fettmilch overthrow the council, seek to introduce a new municipal constitution and expel the Jews. After the rebels have been declared outlaws by Imperial Decree the municipal council is able to re-establish its authority with the support of the more moderate element among the citizens.
1624	Matthäus Merian the Elder takes over the Frankfurt art publishing house of his father-in-law Johann Theodor de Bry (which sells engravings from all over Europe), with the associated copperplate engraving workshops.
From 1627	Construction of new fortifications.
1631–35	Frankfurt is occupied by the Swedes.
1661	Establishment of the first German faience manufactory at Hanau (in 1666 in Frankfurt).
1666	The Protestant theologian Philipp Jakob Spener is called to Frankfurt, which becomes a centre of Lutheran pietism.
1689	Opening of the first coffee-house.
1700/1748	Foundation of the Bethmann Brothers' bank. Frankfurt is now the principal German banking centre, with the banking houses of the Bethmanns, de Neufville, Metzler, Willemer, etc.
1708 (1716?)	Complaints by the citizens about the arbitrary rule of the patrician municipal council lead the Emperor to order an administrative reform which comes into force in 1728:

examination of municipal finances by boards of auditors, new
procedure for electing officials, etc.

Georg Philipp Telemann becomes Musical Director in Frankfurt (until 1721).   1712

Johann Wolfgang Goethe born on 28 August in the family
house in the Hirschgraben. The grandson on his mother's side
of a Mayor of Frankfurt, he thus belongs to one of the town's
most influential families.   1749

Frankfurt is occupied by the French during the Seven Years
War.   1759

Johann Christian Senckenberg founds the Bürgerhospital   1763
(which still exists) and bequeathes his fortune to a scientific
and social foundation (medical institute, botanic garden,
chemical laboratory, etc.), which in 1817 is amalgamated with
the Senckenberg Society for the Study of Nature, originally
established on the initiative of Goethe.

Foundation of the "Frankfurter gelehrte Anzeigen", a literary   1772
and scientific periodical. The 1772 volume is noteworthy for
contributions by Goethe, Herder and others.

Building of the Paulskirche.   1787

Francis II is elected Emperor on 2 July – the last Imperial   1792
election in Frankfurt.
Frankfurt is occupied by French Revolutionary forces commanded by the Comte de Custine, who are driven out again
on 2 December by Hessian and Prussian forces and the
townspeople.

Frankfurt is bombarded and occupied by French forces under   1796
Marshal Jourdan.

The town has a population of some 50,000.   About 1800

The town acquires considerable property following the   1803
secularisation of churches and religious houses.

Demolition of the town's fortifications.   1804–09

Napoleon's Continental Blockade brings substantial economic   1806
advantage to Frankfurt as a result of the elimination of British
competition.
The town loses its status as a free city of the Empire and
becomes the seat of the Electoral Arch-Chancellor and Prince-
Primate of Germany, Karl Theodor von Dalberg.

Karl Theodor von Dalberg is invested with the newly created   1810
Grand Duchy of Frankfurt (Frankfurt, the district of Aschaffenburg, Wetzlar and the principalities of Fulda and Hanau). On
16 December Dalberg promulgates a constitution providing for
an assembly of the Estates, equality of all citizens in the eye of
the law and the abolition of serfdom.

Frankfurt is liberated by Prussian, Austrian and Russian forces. 1813
Dalberg abdicates and the Grand Duchy is dissolved. Frankfurt

again becomes a free city and its previous constitution is restored.

1815	With the establishment of the German Confederation Frankfurt becomes the seat of the Bundestag (the Assembly of the Confederation), which meets in the Palais Thurn und Taxis. The Bundestag, under Austrian presidency, is responsible for all foreign, military and internal affairs of the Confederation.
1816	Under an amendment to the constitution Frankfurt is given a Senate and a Legislative Assembly (until 1866). The Frankfurt banker Johann Friedrich Städel bequeathes his collection and a large sum of money for the foundation of a college of art and a picture gallery – the origin of the Städel Art Institute and College of Art.
1819	Treaty signed by Austria, Prussia, Britain and Russia putting an end to the territorial changes of the Napoleonic period in Germany. The radical liberal economist and politician Friedrich List establishes, with its headquarters in Frankfurt, the General German Commercial and Industrial Union, which seeks to achieve the unity of Greater Germany and opposes the economic particularism (internal customs) of the German Confederation. Rioting, followed by anti-Jewish excesses. Freiherr vom Stein founds the Early German History Society in Frankfurt.
1833	A group of radical students and workmen storm the Hauptwache (Guard-House) in Frankfurt in an attempt to initiate a revolutionary rising against the Metternich system. They receive no support from the public and are quickly overcome by troops. Following this unsuccessful attempt at a *putsch*, Government troops are stationed in the town and persecution of liberals in Germany is intensified (arrests, exclusion from Government employment, etc.).
1836	Frankfurt joins the German Customs Union.
1839	Opening of the Taunusbahn, the first railway line from Frankfurt to the Rhine.
1848	The "German Revolution": March: The Bundestag in Frankfurt adopts the German national colours – black, red and gold. March–April: A Pre-Parliament meets in the Paulskirche in Frankfurt and resolves to summon a German National Assembly to meet there. 18 May: The National Assembly meets in the Paulskirche, with the object of drafting a constitution for a German national state. September: During violent unrest and risings by left-wing radicals two Prussian members of the National Assembly, Felix von Lichnowsky and Major-General Hans von Auerswald, are murdered. In order to take action against left-wing activists the Assembly is compelled to fall back on Prussian, Austrian and other troops, thus revealing its weakness (lack of executive power). 27 December: A Law on the Basic Rights of the German People is promulgated in Frankfurt.

28 March: Adoption of the "Little Germany" Frankfurt   1849
Constitution, providing for a federation of states under the
leadership of Prussia.
28 April: King Frederick William IV of Prussia refuses the
Imperial crown offered him by the National Assembly. This
marks the final collapse of the "German Revolution".
30 May: The rump of the National Assembly resolves to move
from Frankfurt to Stuttgart.

Foundation of the Frankfurter Bank (since 1970 the Berliner   1854
Handelsgesellschaft – Frankfurter Bank).

The German National Union (a "Little Germany" organisation)   1859
is founded in Frankfurt by Hermann Schulze-Delitzsch, Karl
Ludwig Aegidi, Rudolf von Benningsen and others.

The physicist Johann Philipp Reis substantiates his theoretical   1861
paper on "telephony by galvanic current" by a demonstration
of his first telephone at a meeting of the Physics Society in
Frankfurt.

The German Reform Society (a "Great Germany" organisation)   1862
is founded in Frankfurt. Foundation of the Frankfurter
Hypothekenbank, the first private bank specialising in mort-
gages in Germany (and now the largest purely mortgage bank
in the Federal Republic).

Following the war between Prussia and Austria Frankfurt is   1866
annexed by Prussia. The Frankfurt Stock Exchange and the
Frankfurter Bank lose their predominant position in Germany to
Berlin.

The Peace of Frankfurt ends the Franco-Prussian War   1871
(1870–71).

After assassination attempts by anarchists and other subversive   1886
activities by radicals in the industrial conurbations round
Frankfurt with large concentrations of the proletariat, a "lesser
state of siege" is declared in Frankfurt, Hanau, Höchst and the
Upper Taunus district.
Construction of Western Harbour.

Opening of the Central Station.   1888

The industrial district of Bockenheim is incorporated in   1895
Frankfurt.

Franz Adickes, Chief Burgomaster since 1890, introduces   1902
regulations preventing property speculation in new housing
areas. He plays a major part in the development of the city
(improvement of infrastructure, foundation of University,
progressive social policies, development of Eastern Harbour,
etc.).

Opening of University.   1914

November Revolution: strikes in Frankfurt, formation of   1919
Workers' and Soldiers' Councils.

Frankfurt, Darmstadt and three other towns are occupied by   1920

	French troops in response to the dispatch of German troops into the Ruhr (to repress a left-wing rising in reaction to the Kapp *putsch*).
1924	Opening of Rebstock Airport (used by airships as well as planes).
1927	Establishment of the Frankfurt Goethe Prize, to be awarded to "persons whose creative achievement makes them worthy of an honour dedicated to the memory of Goethe".
1928	Höchst, Sindlingen, Zeilsheim, Unterliederbach, Sossenheim, Nied, Griesheim, Schwanheim and Fechenheim are incorporated in the city.
1936	Opening of the Rhine-Main Airport.
1944	March: After suffering heavy air attack since 1943, the old town is completely destroyed by a further attack.
1945	29 March: American forces occupy Frankfurt.
1948–60	Rebuilding of Cathedral, old town and inner city.
1949	Publication of the "Frankfurter Allgemeine Zeitung", in succession to the former "Allgemeine Zeitung".
1963–68	Construction of first section of U-Bahn (underground).
1972	Opening of new airport terminal.
1977	Bergen-Enkheim is incorporated in Frankfurt, giving the city a total area of 249 sq. km (96 sq. miles).
1981	Reopening of the Old Opera House as a concert hall and congress centre.
1982	Ceremonies marking the completion of the Ostzeile on the Römerberg (rebuilt according to the original plans) and the Leinwandhaus. Reconstruction of Zeil pedestrian precinct.

The following is a list of recipients of the Frankfurt Goethe Prize since 1927:

Goethe Prize

1927 Stefan George	1946 Hermann Hesse
1928 Albert Schweitzer	1947 Karl Jaspers
1929 Leopold Ziegler	1948 Fritz von Unruh
1930 Sigmund Freud	1949 Thomas Mann
1931 Richarda Huch	1952 Carl Zuckmayer
1932 Gerhard Hauptmann	1955 Annette Kolb
1933 Hermann Stehr	1958 Carl von Weizsäcker
1934 Hans Pfitzner	1960 Ernst Beutler
1935 Hermann Stegemann	1961 Walter Gropius
1936 Georg Kolbe	1964 Benno Reifenberg
1937 Guido Kolbenheyer	1967 Carlo Schmid
1938 Hans Carossa	1970 Georg Lukács
1939 Karl Bosch	1973 Arno Schmidt
1940 Agnes Miegel	1976 Ingmar Bergman
1941 Wilhelm Schäfer	1979 Raymond Aron
1942 Richard Kuhn	1982 Ernst Jünger
1945 Max Planck	

Sights from A to Z

Airport

See Rhine-Main Airport

* Alt-Sachsenhausen (Old Sachsenhausen) K16/17 (C/D25/26)

Buses
36, 960 (Elisabethenstrasse)

Trams
11, 13, 16
(Frankensteiner Platz)

Legend has it that Sachsenhausen was founded by Charlemagne, who is said to have resettled families of the defeated Saxons here. It first appears in the records in 1193, and is referred to in 1318 as belonging to Frankfurt. In the years following 1390 it was surrounded by walls, of which only the Kuhhirtenturm (see entry; 1490) now survives.
The walls enclosed a triangular area, still broadly marked out by the river-bank between the Iron Bridge (see entry) and the Upper Main Bridge, Dreieichstrasse, Neuer Wall, Wallstrasse and Schulstrasse.

Ebbelwei quarter

The closely packed half-timbered houses of Alt-Sachsenhausen – still mainly occupied by craftsmen and other manual workers in the first half of the 20th c. – form a picturesquely medieval setting for the Ebbelwei quarter (cider quarter), now a district of pseudo-historical character dedicated to the entertainment of tourists.
The medieval fortified gates of Sachsenhausen were replaced in 1810–11 by a neo-classical guard-house (designed by Johann Friedrich Christian Hess) in Affentorplatz, which was originally circular in plan.
From here the late 19th c. part of Sachsenhausen extends south and west, centred on the Schweizer Strasse.

Applied Arts, Museum of

See Museum of Applied Arts

Architecture, Museum of

See German Museum of Architecture

Bad Vilbel – Moated Castle A21

Location
D-6368 Bad Vilbel

S-Bahn
S 6 (Bad Vilbel)

The ruins of the moated castle lie on the right bank of the Nidda in the old town of Bad Vilbel.
The castle, the oldest parts of which are thought to date from the 12th c., was surrounded by a circuit of walls, a hall, a corner tower, a gate tower, domestic offices and working quarters, and a moat linked with the Nidda. In the 14th c. it was held by the

A picturesque corner in Alt-Sachsenhausen

knightly Vilbel family. In 1399 the castle was destroyed by a force from Frankfurt, Hanau and Falkenstein, which had been under the threat of constant attack by Bechtram V, and this robber knight was finally executed in Frankfurt in 1420. In 1409–14 the castle was rebuilt by Werner von Falkenstein, Archbishop of Trier, and the present entrance gate still bears his coat of arms, with the cross of Trier and the wheel of Mainz. The castle was held by the Falkenstein family until 1539, and from 1580 to 1803 it belonged to the Archbishop-Elector of Mainz. It was finally destroyed in 1790 during the French Revolutionary Wars. In 1955 it became the property of the town of Bad Ibel, which restored the tower and used it to house a local museum. Open-air performances are put on in the castle courtyard.

Banking District (Bankenviertel)   J15/16 (A/B23)

Frankfurt's development into a commercial and financial metropolis began with its medieval fairs, which brought currency from many different countries into the town. Money-dealers and traders established private banks (Bethmann, Grunelius, Metzler), some of which still exist. During the 19th c. the financing of railway construction and of wars increased Frankfurt's prosperity; but after the establishment of the German Empire in 1871 Berlin displaced it as Germany's leading financial centre.

After the Second World War the situation changed again, and Frankfurt developed into the financial centre of the German

Location
Westend

Federal Republic. A decisive step in this development was the establishment in Frankfurt of the Bank Deutscher Länder, the predecessor of the German Federal Bank, which was attracted to the city by the proximity of the Notenbank and the Frankfurt Stock Exchange as well as the convenient geographical situation. Apart from the German Federal Bank and the Central Provincial Bank of Hessen there are now 346 credit institutions with headquarters, subsidiaries or branches in Frankfurt, including 196 foreign banks (120 agencies and 76 subsidiaries or branches), all in what is known as the Banking District (Bankenviertel), the western part of the city centre, extending beyond the Wallanlagen (see entry), and on the Bockenheimer Landstrasse in Westend (see entry). The many high-rise blocks (see entry) in this part of the city have given Frankfurt the nickname of Mainhattan or Chicago on the Main (appropriately, since Frankfurt is twinned with Chicago). Although Frankfurt can vie with Paris, Amsterdam and Zürich as a financial centre, however, it cannot compete with London and New York as the dominant financial centres of the Western World.

Beethoven Monument

See Wallanlagen

Bergen-Enkheim

D–F21–23

Location
10 km (6 miles) NE of Frankfurt city centre

Bus
43

Trams
18, 20

The communes of Bergen and Enkheim were amalgamated in 1936, and were granted a municipal charter in 1968; in 1977, however, the town was incorporated in Frankfurt. The old town of half-timbered houses, predominantly in Baroque style, was originally surrounded by walls (1440), with ten towers and gates on the east and west sides. Of these fortifications there survive the White Tower (1472) in Gangstrasse and parts of the walls (Im Sperber, Conrad-Weil-Gasse). After the Seven Years War (1756–63) the walls were used as a source of building material, and when Bergen became Prussian in 1866 they finally lost any defensive significance.

Old Town Hall

The central feature of the town was the Old Town Hall in Marktstrasse. A stone building in Gothic style was erected in the first half of the 14th c. as a court-house and market hall; then during the Renaissance, in 1520–30, the building was given a half-timbered superstructure and used as a town hall; and in 1704 it was enlarged in Baroque style. Since 1959 it has housed a local museum (Heimatmuseum).

Heimatmuseum

Built into the west side of the Town Hall is a stone slab known as the Fratzenstein (1479), with a Late Gothic carved head and the inscription "Far, du Gauch" ("Off you go, you fool") – a warning to vagrants and travelling entertainers to keep out of the town.

Schelmenburg

Also in Marktstrasse (No. 13) is a house known as the Schelmenburg, now occupied by municipal offices. It stands

In the Banking District of Frankfurt, financial centre of West Germany ▶

Heimatmuseum in the Old Town Hall, Bergen

on the site of a Roman fort, and is known to have belonged to the Schelm family of Bergen as early as 1194. The Schelms soon became vassals of the Counts of Hanau, who gained control of Bergen in 1279 and enlarged their estates at the expense of other landowners. Thereafter they preyed on passing merchants; but in 1380/81 a force from Frankfurt occupied the Schelm castle and put an end to the activities of these robber knights.

During the 14th and 15th c. the Counts of Hanau contrived to incorporate much of Bergen in their family estates. The Schelms lost all influence: the time of the knights had passed. Property-holders gradually acquired full ownership of land previously held as fiefs, and the last feudal obligations disappeared with the end of the Holy Roman Empire in 1806. The Schelmenburg was demolished down to the basement and rebuilt in Baroque style, though the outer moat was retained. The Schelms of Bergen finally died out in 1844.

There is a story that one of the Schelms of Bergen was a hangman who danced, unrecognised, with the Empress of Frederick Barbarossa: whereupon, to avert the ill-fortune which it was feared might follow, he was ennobled by the Emperor. The legend inspired a poem by Heinrich Heine.

Nikolauskapelle

Near the Town Hall is the Nikolauskapelle (St Nicholas's Chapel), built in 1524, replacing an earlier chapel, for the Cistercian Abbey of Haina. The chapel stood within a royal stronghold, part of which was presented to the abbey in 1220 by the Emperor Frederick II.

The abbey property, the Hainer Hof, extended as far as the town walls, beyond which was a vineyard reaching to the Enkeimer

Mönchof (1771–74; Riedstrasse 95–97). The old Court-House (1864; Am Königshof 5) stands on the site of a house which provided lodging for the monks sent to Bergen to work in the vineyard and the fields.

The original chapel and its Late Gothic successor of 1524 were built for these monks. The new chapel, however, soon fell, after the Reformation, into the hands of the Landgrave of Hessen, and later passed to Hessen–Darmstadt. In 1818, after the union of the Reformed and Lutheran Churches, it was secularised and fell into private ownership. It is still used as a store.

The Protestant Church of Bergen, adjoining the town walls, was built in 1684, replacing an earlier church which had long fallen into ruin. The tower was heightened in 1741–43.

Protestant church, Bergen

The Protestant Parish Church of Enkheim in the 16th c. was St Lawrence's (St. Laurentius), a church first recorded in 1445. It was replaced in 1717–19 by the present Baroque church.

Protestant church, Enkheim

North-west of Bergen, on the Vilbeler Landstrasse, is the Berger Warte, a tower which first appears in the records in 1340 as the Geierswarte (Vulture's Tower).

Berger Warte

In 1552, during the War of the League of Schmalkalden, the original half-timbered tower was burned down, and in 1557 it was rebuilt in stone.

The tower was originally entered by a small door which could be reached only with the help of a ladder. The present external staircase was built in 1844, using stone from an old gallows which stood here.

Since 1972 Bergen-Enkheim has annually appointed a writer to serve as "Town Clerk of Bergen-Enkheim" – a post which attracts an honorarium but involves no duties.

"Town Clerk of Bergen-Enkheim"

Berger Warte

See under Bergen-Enkheim

Bethmannhof

The Bethmannhof, at the corner of Buchgasse and Bethmannstrasse, is the headquarters of the Gebrüder Bethmann's banking house which was founded by Simon Moritz von Bethmann in 1748 and which established the international standing of the Frankfurt Stock Exchange (see entry) in the 18th c. it is still the largest private bank in Hessen.

Location
Bethmannstrasse 7–9

Trams
13, 14, 15, 16, 18
(Paulskirche)

The Bethmann family have been munificent benefactors of Frankfurt, promoting its cultural life and social welfare services. The house which they acquired in 1762, known as the Basler Hof, was given its present name only after its rebuilding in 1948. Another house, Zum Strauss, which was acquired by the family in 1818 and pulled down in 1896, is commemorated by a representation of the house in the walled-up gateway adjoining the west wing of the Bethmannhof. Luther is said to have spent the night in this house in 1521 on his way to the Diet of Worms.

The gateway at Buchgasse 9 dates from the late 17th c. The door and railings are modern.

"Bethmännchen"

Marzipan balls, with half almonds set into the sides, are known in Frankfurt as "Bethmännchen" (*männchen* = "little man"). The story goes that there were originally four pieces of almond, representing the four sons of Simon Moritz von Bethmann, and that after the death of his son Heinrich in 1845 the number was reduced to three.

Bethmann Park

See Wallanlagen

Bockenheimer Anlage

See Wallanlagen

Bockenheimer Warte   H14

Location
Bockenheimer Landstrasse

Trams
17, 19, 21, 22
(Bockenheimer Warte)

The Bockenheimer Warte (1434–35), on the road to Bockenheim, is one of the four Late Gothic watch-towers which reinforced the town's medieval outer defences. The construction of this defensive earthwork, at a distance of up to 2·5 km (1½ miles) outside the town walls, was resolved upon in 1393 as a means of protecting the area round the town from the constant threat of attack by robber knights. The original wooden towers were replaced by stone towers defending the main road from 1414 onwards during the process of strengthening the town's defences. The new defensive system was completed in 1481.

The line of the defences can now be identified only by careful study of the topography, but the watch-towers are still in existence. They now house ventilation shafts for the city's sewers. Only the Sachsenhäuser Warte (see entry) is still occupied.

Bonames   A/B15/16

Location
10 km (6 miles) N of
Frankfurt city centre

U-Bahn
U 2 (Bonames-Mitte)

The former village of Bonames lies to the north-east of Frankfurt on the Nidda. The name, thought to be derived from *bona mansio*, first appears in the records in 1059. Archaeological evidence has confirmed the antiquity of settlement on this site.

Bonames, situated on an old trade route into the Wetterau, became a free city of the Empire in 1367. It was surrounded with a Late Gothic defensive wall on a polygonal plan, with two gateways and eleven towers, in 1413, at the same time as Frankfurt's outer defensive line was constructed. To facilitate the collection of tolls an earlier wooden bridge over the Nidda was replaced by a stone bridge with a removable barrier (rebuilt 1482, widened 1892).

After the construction of the Friedberger Warte (see entry) in 1478 Bonames declined in importance, since commercial traffic now preferred to use the Friedberger Landstrasse. Thereafter the town walls and the castle to the west of the town were used by the local peasants as sources of good stone, and only the northern part of the walls, the round tower of the lower gateway and the south-eastern corner tower survived. The stone bridge still exists, but has lost its function with the realignment and subsequent silting-up of the Nidda (1961).

To the north of the bridge, adjoining a corner tower which formed part of the town's medieval defences, is a neo-classical country house, created about 1830 for a member of the Metzler banking family by the conversion of an earlier Baroque building. It occupies the site of the medieval Saalhof. The garden was laid out by Sebastian Rinz.

The Baroque church in the town centre dates from 1642. It was a rebuilding of the Late Gothic parish church, which itself had replaced an earlier church outside the town walls.

Bornheim G19

Bornheim is the most populous part of Frankfurt. From 1475 to 1866 it was a village, which was incorporated in the town in 1877. The nucleus of the old village can still be identified in the Johanniskirche (St John's Church), a Baroque structure with an onion-domed tower which was built as a parish church in 1752–53 and rebuilt by Johann Andreas Liebhardt in 1778–81 after a fire, and in a number of half-timbered houses round the church. In the Berger Strasse, a pedestrian shopping precinct popularly called the Bernemer Zeil, are the Hoher Brunnen (High Fountain), an obelisk designed by Philipp Jakob Hoffmann (1827) for the public water supply, and the old Town Hall (No. 314), a Baroque half-timbered building now a dwelling-house. The square at the intersection of Berger Strasse and Arnsburger Strasse, with a small clock-tower, is occupied on Wednesdays and Saturdays by a market.

On the Bornheimer Hang is a housing scheme (by Ernst May, 1926–29) in the functional style known as Neue Sachlichkeit, with the Heiligkreuzkirche (by Martin Weber, 1928–29; Wittelsbacher Allee 203–205) and the Hallgartenschule (1929–30).

U-Bahn
U 4 (Bornheim-Mitte)

Trams
12, 15

Carmelite Friary (Municipal Archives) K16 (C24)

The Carmelite Friary, founded in 1246, occupies an area bounded by Münzgasse, Seckbächergasse, Alte Mainzer Gasse and Karmelitergasse. A simple aisleless church was consecrated in 1270, and this was followed by a rectangular choir completed in 1290. The purchase of additional land made it possible to begin work on the south transept about 1300. Donations by Frankfurt patricians, including the Holzhausen family, enabled the choir to be raised and vaulted over about 1430. About 1450 the south transept was given a west aisle by the amalgamation of a number of chapels, and the side facing the Alte Mainzer Gasse became the main front.

The friary extended to the north of the church in two parallel

Location
Karmelitergasse 5

U-Bahn
U 1–4 (Theaterplatz)

Trams
13, 14, 15, 16, 18
(Paulskirche)

Opening times
Mon.–Fri. 8 a.m.–4 p.m.

Carmelite Friary

The Municipal Archives . . .

. . . in the Carmelite Friary

ranges, with the refectory (1517; paintings by Jörg Ratgeb) and the cloister (1523). After its secularisation the friary was used for other purposes, and in 1913 was threatened with demolition. It was restored between 1922 and 1943, and further restoration work was necessary after the Second World War.

The conventual buildings were rebuilt in 1955–57, and most of them are now occupied by the Municipal Archives, documents and mementoes relating to the history of Frankfurt being housed in new underground store-rooms. The material dates back to the 9th c. and includes documents relating to the Cathedral (see entry) and religious houses in the town. One of the greatest treasures is the copy of the Golden Bull (see History, p. 22) made for Frankfurt in 1366.

Municipal Archives

Associated with the Municipal Archives are the Association for Historical and Regional Studies and the Frankfurt Historical Commission. Special exhibitions by the Museum of Applied Arts (see entry) are put on in the main building. The wing facing on to Seckbächer Gasse houses the Frankfurt section of the Federal Archives.

The Association of Professional Artists has studios and exhibition rooms in the building, and in the basement there are performances by the "Schmiere", "the worst theatre in the world".

In 1975–77 the refectory, Frankfurt's finest Renaissance room, was restored and the cloister was glassed in to protect its tempera paintings. The earlier cycle of paintings, executed between 1514 and 1517 by Jörg Ratgeb (born *c.* 1480 at Herrenberg in Württemberg), depict the history of the Carmelite Order. A later cycle by the same artist, depicting Christ's Nativity and Passion, is the most extensive series of wall-paintings of the transitional period between the Middle Ages and modern times to be found north of the Alps. The paintings, which are badly damaged, are at present being restored.

Refectory and cloister

Not long after completing these paintings Jörg Ratgeb was hanged, drawn and quartered at Pforzheim in 1526 as one of the ringleaders of a peasant rising which was successfully quashed by the Swabian League.

The friary church is being incorporated in the new Museum of Prehistory (Holzhausenschlösschen, see entry), to the design of Josef Paul Kleihus, winner of an architectural competition in 1980.

Church

---

*Cathedral (Dom)   J/K17 (C25)

The former collegiate and parish church which has been known since medieval times as the Cathedral became in 1356, by Imperial Decree, the place of election of German kings and in 1562 the place of coronation of the Emperor. Thereafter it held the status of an "Imperial Cathedral" (Kaiserdom).

The Gothic tower and spire are a dominant feature of the old town and afford good views over the city.

The present church is the successor to the earlier Church of St Salvator which was founded by Ludwig (Louis) the German

Location
Domplatz

U-Bahn
U 4 (Römer)

Trams
13, 14, 15, 16, 18
(Domstrasse)

Cathedral

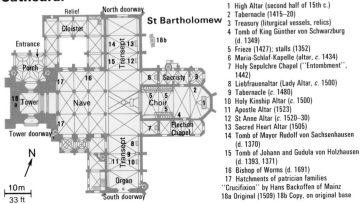

Relief North doorway St Bartholomew

Cloister

Entrance

Porch

Tower Nave

Tower doorway

N

10m
33 ft

Sacristy

Choir

Election Chapel

Organ

South doorway

1 High Altar (second half of 15th c.)
2 Tabernacle (1415–20)
3 Treasury (liturgical vessels, relics)
4 Tomb of King Günther von Schwarzburg (d. 1349)
5 Frieze (1427); stalls (1352)
6 Maria-Schlaf-Kapelle (altar, c. 1434)
7 Holy Sepulchre Chapel ("Entombment", 1442)
8 Liebfrauenaltar (Lady Altar, c. 1500)
9 Tabernacle (c. 1480)
10 Holy Kinship Altar (c. 1500)
11 Apostle Altar (1523)
12 St Anne Altar (c. 1520–30)
13 Sacred Heart Altar (1505)
14 Tomb of Mayor Rudolf von Sachsenhausen (d. 1370)
15 Tomb of Johann and Gudula von Holzhausen (d. 1393, 1371)
16 Bishop of Worms (d. 1691)
17 Hatchments of patrician families
"Crucifixion" by Hans Backoffen of Mainz
18a Original (1509) 18b Copy, on original base

after 840 and probably consecrated in 852. After major restoration work at the beginning of the 13th c. the church was re-dedicated to St Bartholomew.

Constructional history

In 1248 the nave was replaced by a new one of hall-church type – one of the earliest in Hessen. A new choir (involving the rebuilding of the Carolingian apse) was begun in 1315 and consecrated in 1349. A series of square chapels (1355) were built on to the south side of the choir, the sacristy on the north side; above the chapels was the Election Chapel (completed 1436), above the sacristy the chapter house. The Carolingian transept was pulled down in 1348 and a new one was built, each arm being longer than the nave. The ground-plan of the church thus took on the form of a cross with arms of equal length.

Tower

The church originally had two towers, mainly Carolingian work, which were out of proportion with the Gothic cathedral. These were demolished, and in 1415 a beginning was made with the construction of the present west tower (known as the Pfarrturm or Parish Tower), to the design of Madern Gerthener. By the time of Gerthener's death in 1430/31 the tower had been carried up as far as the transition from the square base to the octagonal shaft, and under his successors, over a period of almost a hundred years, it was completed as far as the cupola. The decorative elements and the octagonal lantern topping the tower were added only in 1877, ten years after a fire which caused serious damage; the work was done under the direction of the Cathedral Architect, Franz Josef von Denzinger, to Gerthener's original plans. The nave was now heightened to match the transept. A porch and an entrance chapel, named after Denzinger, were added on the north side of the tower, involving the demolition of the west side of the cloister. In the same year (1877) new bells were installed.

Cathedral, Saalhof and Mainkai ▶

St Bartholomew frieze (15th c.)

Adjoining the Cathedral on the north-east was the churchyard, enclosed by a wall, with a Crucifixion group by Hans Backoffen (original now inside the Cathedral). The coronation procession entered the Cathedral by the north doorway, and the ceremony took place under the crossing.

The Cathedral suffered damage during the Second World War, and was restored between 1948 and 1953, sacrificing the 19th c. wall-paintings by Steinle (1882–90).

Interior furnishings

The Cathedral was never exposed to serious damage by Protestant iconoclasts, and still preserves a number of Gothic features. During the 17th and 18th c., however, many works of art were removed and replaced by works in Baroque style.

Surviving original features are the Maria-Schlaf-Altar (Death of the Virgin Altar, *c.* 1434); the rather later Heilig-Grab-Altar (Holy Sepulchre Altar); the St Bartholomew frieze (begun 1427) and the carved stalls (1352) in the choir; the Tomb of King Günther von Schwarzburg on the south wall of the choir; and the gravestone of Burgomaster Johann von Holzhausen and his wife Gudula Goldstein in the north transept.

At the west end of the north aisle are the hatchments of Frankfurt patricians of the 14th–16th c.

Central Market Hall (Grossmarkthalle) K18 (C27)

Location
Rückertstrasse, Ostend

The Central Market Hall, designed by Martin Elsaesser, was built in 1927–28 as a replacement for the Little Market (1879; see entry) in Hasengasse. A reinforced-concrete structure

The Central Station: architecture typical of the 1880s

faced with clinker brick, it has a concrete roof of 15 barrel-shaped sections only 7·5 cm (3 in) thick at their highest point, without intermediate supports, and is flanked by two towers containing offices and cold stores. Covering an area 250 m (820 ft) by 50 m (164 ft), it is one of the largest buildings of its kind in Germany. Some 160 producers, 115 wholesalers and 30 importers are represented in the market, and another 70 firms are associated with it. The convenient situation of the market between a main road and the railway and its proximity to the business quarter of Frankfurt make for a rapid turnover of goods. The market starts about 5 in the morning and ends about 11. The building also houses the municipal kitchens.

There is a special market for flowers at the Friedberger Warte (see entry).

Trams
11, 14, 18 (Bärenstrasse)

Opening times
Mon.–Fri. 5–11 a.m.

---

* **Central Station** (Hauptbahnhof) K15 (C/D22/23)

In the course of half a century of rapid railway development the goods traffic handled in Frankfurt increased from its original level of 50,000 tons a year to something like 50 times as much, and there was a similar increase in passenger traffic. The original terminus stations of the various railway lines serving the town – the Taunusbahn (1838), the Main–Weser-Bahn (1852), the Main–Neckar-Bahn (1848) – could not cope with this enormously increased traffic; and the movement of troops by rail during the Franco-Prussian War had strikingly revealed the inadequacies of the stations serving the west. The plan for building a Central Station which was put before the municipal

U-Bahn
U 4 (Hauptbahnhof)

S-Bahn
S 1–8, S 11–14
(Hauptbahnhof)

Trams
10, 11, 13, 14, 15, 16, 18
(Hauptbahnhof)

parliament in 1875 followed the purchase by the Prussian Government of most of the private railway companies; and after preliminary technical studies a competition was held in 1880, in which the leading German architects of the day submitted designs, most of them influenced by classical models. The winning design was submitted by an architect named Eggert, and the new station was built under his direction between 1883 and 1888. It was then the largest of its type, not exceeded in size until the construction of a new Central Station in Leipzig in 1915.

Terminus building

The monumental terminus building with its imposing sand-stone façade is strikingly articulated by the projecting ticket hall and the tower-like corner pavilions, and the effect is enhanced by the rich sculptural decoration. On the highest point of the ticket hall is an Atlas group by Franz Krüger; the clock is flanked by figures representing Morning and Evening; and there are also allegorical representations of Commerce and Transport and a series of figures depicting different types of passenger, from the honeymooner to the educational tripper. Among the sculptors were Hundrieser, Herold, Kaupert, Krüger and Schierholz.

Platform shed

The platform shed, 168 m (551 ft) long, is made up of three aisles each 56 m (184 ft) wide. The roof structure, with its three-jointed trusses rising to a height of 28·5 m (94 ft) above the platforms, was designed by an architect named Schwedler, who had gained his experience in the spanning of larger areas in the construction of gasometers and Berlin railway stations. Originally built to house 18 lines, the shed was enlarged in 1924 by the addition of two aisles each containing three lines. Under the north end of the station is an underground station, an interchange point for the U-Bahn and S-Bahn, with a shopping arcade.

Deutschherrnbrücke (Bridge of the Teutonic Knights)   K18

Bus
46 (Rudererdorf)

When the Eastern Harbour (see entry) was constructed in the early years of the 20th c. a plan which had previously been considered in the latter part of the 19th c. for linking the railway lines on the right and left banks of the Main at the east end of the town was also put into effect. The steel truss structure of the Deutschherrnbrücke, a railway bridge with a passage for pedestrians built in 1911–13 at a cost of 469,000 marks, forms a striking conclusion to the vista along the banks of the Main to the east.

Deutschordenshaus (House of the Teutonic Order)   K17 (C26)

Location
Brückenstrasse 3–7

Buses
36, 960 (Elisabethenstrasse)

The former House of the Teutonic Order, a Baroque structure with three wings designed by Daniel Kayser, was built between 1709 and 1715 on the foundations of an earlier Gothic building, with a history going back to a hospice founded by Kuno von Münzenberg before 1193 and presented to the Teutonic Order by the Emperor Frederick II in 1221. The doorway (1714–15) was designed by Maximilian von Welsch,

The Baroque House of the Teutonic Order

Architect to the Archbishop of Mainz. The building was destroyed during the war and rebuilt with some alterations in 1963–65. Original features are a figure of the Virgin by Bernhard Schwarzburger at the north-west corner, figures of knights by Erich Neuberger of Idstein (*c.* 1715; heads restored 1975) above the main entrance, a range of residential quarters in the south courtyard remodelled in Baroque style, with coats of arms of 1565, and, on the neo-Gothic presbytery, a capital of the Staufen period from the earliest chapel (*c.* 1200).

Here in the 14th c. an unknown priest wrote a treatise "On the Perfect Life" which Martin Luther published in 1516 under the title "A German Theology" – the book which he most treasured after the Bible.

The building returned to the hands of the Teutonic Order in 1958. In addition to the rooms used by the Order, including the Knights' Hall, it houses a students' residence, the municipal department concerned with the arts and sciences and the Communal Gallery, which puts on exhibitions of work by artists living in Frankfurt.

On the ground floor is the Roman Exhibition (opened 1976) organised by the Museum of Prehistory and Early History, with a collection of architectural fragments and everyday objects which gives a comprehensive view of the Roman settlement of Nida, near Heddernheim, which existed from A.D. 75 to 250. (For opening times inquire by telephone – 5 12 50 31.)

St Mary's Church (St. Maria), which belonged to the original hospice, is believed to have been founded in 1309. The interior is aisleless, with ribbed vaulting; notable features are the Late

Opening times
Communal Gallery
Mon., Tue., Thu. and Fri.
9 a.m.–5 p.m., Wed.
9 a.m.–8 p.m.

Communal Gallery

Roman Exhibition

St Mary's Church

Gothic side altars, by unknown masters, and a work of Gothic sculpture in wood, "Beheading of John the Baptist".
The provision of a new Baroque façade for the church (by Ferdinand Kirchmeyer, 1747–51, for Elector Clemens August of Cologne) to match the Deutschordenshaus gave Frankfurt its earliest and most effective architectural ensemble of the Baroque period.

Diamond Exchange (Diamantbörse)   J17 (B25)

Location
Stephanstrasse 3

Tram
12 (Stephanstrasse)

Opposite the Petersfriedhof (St Peter's Cemetery; see entry) is the former Diamond Exchange, built in 1971–74 (architect Richard Heil) as a new "market-place" for diamonds. But it was unable to compete with the older markets dealing in precious stones – partly because the diamond-cutting workshops were not in Frankfurt – and the Exchange closed in 1976.
The building is now occupied by shops, travel agencies and the East–West Trading Bank of the Soviet Union.

Dominican Friary and Church of the Holy Ghost
(Dominikanerkloster, Heilig-Geist-Kirche)   J17 (B26)

Location
Kurt-Schumacher-Strasse 23

Buses
36, 960 (Börneplatz)

Trams
13, 14, 15, 16, 18
(Börneplatz)

Church of the Holy Ghost

Opening times
By previous arrangement with the porter of the Regional Evangelical Union (tel. 2 16 51)

The Dominican Friary, which was destroyed during the Second World War and rebuilt between 1954 and 1958, stands at the corner of Battonnstrasse and Kurt-Schumacher-Strasse.
The buildings are now occupied by the offices of the Frankfurt Regional Union of the Evangelical (Protestant) Church and are used for meetings and conferences of the German Evangelical Church.

The Dominicans – the first Monastic Order to come to Frankfurt – established themselves here, on the east side of the town just inside the Staufen walls (see entry), in 1233. The Church of the Holy Ghost was consecrated in 1259, and from 1261 served as the burial church for the Frankfurt patriciate. With the help of donations from wealthy citizens the building was given a vaulted roof (1449), designed by Jörg Östreicher, who also built the choir (which still survives). Thanks to the munificence of Frankfurt patricians the church had the most valuable furnishings of any of the town's medieval churches; but with the coming of the Reformation their donations were much reduced. A modest revival of interest in a later period is reflected in the arcades of the Baroque cloister.
After the secularisation of religious houses the conventual buildings were used as a warehouse and a school, while the church served as a gymnasium – which at any rate preserved the buildings from demolition. The church, rebuilt in 1957–61, now has a simple timber roof over the aisled nave; Jörg Östreicher's choir (1470 onwards) has ribbed vaulting. The altar, pulpit and font are modern.
The most important works of art from the friary are now distributed among Frankfurt's museums. The Städel (see entry) has the high altar, by Hans Holbein the Elder, and the altar-pieces by Hans Baldung Grien, while the Historical Museum (see entry) has the side panels, by Matthias Grünewald, of the

Heller Altar; the central panel of this altar, Dürer's "Assumption and Coronation of the Virgin" (1509), was destroyed in a fire in the Residenz in Munich in 1673.
Concerts (including a series of recitals of older music) are given in the cloister in summer.

Dreikönigskirche (Church of the Three Kings)   K17 (C25)

The skyline of the Sachsenhäuser Ufer, on the south bank of the Main, is dominated by the 80 m (260 ft) high spire of the neo-Gothic Church of the Three Kings. The site was originally occupied by a hospice chapel founded by a Frankfurt citizen named Heile Diemar and consecrated to the Three Kings in 1340. In 1452 this became the parish church of Sachsenhausen, and from 1531 it was used for Protestant worship. Later it fell into a state of dilapidation, until in the 19th c. it was pulled down and replaced (1875–81) by a new church designed by Franz Josef von Denzinger, who was also responsible for the completion of the Cathedral (see entry).
This was the first major neo-Gothic church built in Frankfurt, in a style modelled on the city's Late Gothic churches. It has a polygonal apse and a choir and nave of equal width; of the five bays of the nave three are flanked by aisles of the same height.

Location
Sachsenhäuser Ufer

Buses
46, 961, 963, 972, 973
(Eiserner Steg)
36, 960 (Elisabethenstrasse)

Near the church, between Dreikönigsstrasse and Oppenheimer Strasse 5, is a neo-classical fountain topped by a sculpture of the Three Kings. It was set up here in 1781, replacing a medieval well.

Fountain

Eastern Harbour (Osthafen)   J/K19/20

The Eastern Harbour, designed by the municipal civil engineering department, was constructed in 1909–12 as a replacement for the Western Harbour, which was no longer capable of coping with the steadily increasing freight traffic on the Main. At the same time a considerable area of land between the Ostend and Fechenheim districts of Frankfurt was opened up to provide urgently needed sites for industrial development – an area which has proved sufficient to meet industrial needs down to the present day.

Location
Hanauer Landstrasse,
Honsellstrasse,
Schielestrasse

S-Bahn
S 7 (Ostbahnhof)

Trams
11, 14, 18
(Osthafenplatz)

Bus
31 (Honsellbrücke)

The western entrance to the harbour is spanned by the Honsell Bridge, the first stage of a planned two-level bridge over the Main to link the Alleenring and the Sachsenhäuser Ufer. A notable feature of the bridge, apart from its sickle-arched structure, is the generously planned approach ramp with its relief-decorated basalt parapets and a few surviving Art Nouveau street lamps.

Honsell Bridge

The Hanauer Landstrasse between the East Station (Ostbahnhof) and the Kaiserlei roundabout still preserves many handsome shops and office buildings dating from between

Hanauer Landstrasse

1909 and 1914 which have survived the war and the post-war period.

Gasworks

The most striking architectural feature of the Eastern Harbour is the Gasworks, built by Peter Behrens in 1910–12 for the Frankfurt Gas Company. The complex, in neo-classical style, comprises, in addition to the purely industrial requirements (workshops, retort house, regulator house, machine shed, gasholders, etc.), houses for the manager and engineers, offices and a coach-house.

All the buildings in the complex are notable for their close relation between function and form; and their high structural quality is matched by the treatment of details and the choice of materials (purplish-brown iron clinker combined with leather-yellow facing bricks). Striking, too, are the gasholders – originally three in number but now reduced to one squat cylinder with a flat-topped projecting bell for tar and ammonia liquor and the taller and more slender water-tower with a base in the form of a reversed cushion capital.

Eastern Park

See Ostpark

Eiserner Steg

See Iron Bridge

Eschenheim Gardens (Eschenheimer Anlage)

See Wallanlagen

*Eschenheim Tower (Eschenheimer Turm)   J16 (A25)

Location
400 m (440 yd) N of
Hauptwache

U-Bahn
U 1–3 (Eschenheimer Tor)

The Eschenheim Tower (47 m (154 ft) high), one of the finest Late Gothic gate towers in Germany, was built between 1400 and 1428 to replace an earlier tower dating from 1346. It formed part of a medieval defensive system consisting of a moat, a circuit of walls and an outer ward, the gates being further protected by stronger towers, bridges and outworks.

During the Thirty Years War, from 1628 onwards, the fortifications of the town were strengthened by Wilhelm Dillich. Demolition of the walls was begun in 1804 during the reign of the Prince-Primate, Karl von Dalberg, but the Eschenheim Tower was saved by the intervention of the French Ambassador, Hédouville.

The tower was built by the Cathedral Architect, Madern Gerthener. On the inner side of the tower, on the arch below the sentry-walk, is a portrait head, presumably representing Gerthener, and above the sentry-walk is Frankfurt's heraldic eagle, carved by Gerthener. On the outer side, above twin turrets, is a sandstone relief of the two-headed Imperial eagle. The tower is topped by a gilded weather-vane with nine holes

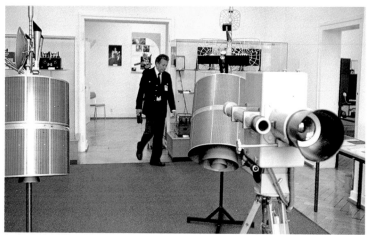

In the Federal Postal Museum

on a basalt base – traditionally said to have been made by a poacher named Hans Winkelsee, who thus purchased his life and escaped execution.

Ethnology, Museum of

See Museum of Ethnology

Federal Postal Museum (Bundespostmuseum)   K16 (D24)

The origins of the Federal Postal Museum go back to 1872, when Heinrich von Stephan, then Postmaster-General, established a Cabinet of Plans and Models in Berlin. This developed into a Postal Museum, which opened its doors to the public in 1878.

The Federal Postal Museum, which opened in Frankfurt in 1958, is housed in the Villa Neufville (designed by Franz von Hoven). It contains most of the material from the earlier Postal Museum, which was evacuated from Berlin during the Second World War, supplemented by later acquisitions. In addition to an introduction to the history of the postal service it offers a series of special displays illustrating the development of postal equipment of all kinds – uniforms, post-horns, letter-boxes, signs, etc. From Philipp Reis's first telephone (1861), the first valve receiver and the first television sets to the transmission of information by laser technology the museum gives an illuminating picture of the development of postal methods and postal apparatus.

For philatelists and stamp-collecting enthusiasts there are interesting special exhibitions every two months, each displaying some 4000 stamps.

Location
Schaumainkai 53

Bus
46 (Städel)

Trams
11, 17, 21, 22
(Schweizer Strasse/
Gartenstrasse)

Opening times
Tue.–Sun. 10 a.m.–7 p.m.

Film Museum

See German Film Museum

Frankfurter Hof (Hotel)   K16 (C24)

Location
Am Kaiserplatz 17

U-Bahn
U 1–4 (Theaterplatz)

Trams
13, 14, 15, 16, 17, 18, 21, 22
(Theaterplatz)

After the decision by the Frankfurt municipal authorities in
1871 to drive a new street through older property from the
Rossmarkt to the railway stations a company was formed, with
municipal support, to build a large new hotel; and in 1875–76
the Frankfurter Hof, designed by Carl Jonas Mylius and
Friedrich Albert Bluntschli (both pupils of Gottfried Semper of
Zürich), was built at the corner of Kaiserstrasse and Bethmannstrasse. The hotel cost 4·7 million gold marks and achieved an
effect of great magnificence both externally and internally.
Built on an H-shaped plan, it has a lavishly decorated façade of
naigreen Palatinate sandstone in the style of the High Renaissance. The forecourt formed by the two projecting side wings
is laid out in gardens, bounded on the street side, facing the
Kaiserplatz, by a colonnade.
The Frankfurter Hof was destroyed during the Second World
War, but by 1948 was again in business. It now has a total of
600 beds.

Imperial Fountain
(Kaiserbrunnen)

Opposite the hotel is the Imperial Fountain (Kaiserbrunnen),
erected in 1876 at the expense of Baron Raphaël d'Erlanger.

Frauen-Friedens-Kirche

See Women's Peace Church

Freedom Fountain (Freiheitsbrunnen)   J17 (C26)

Location
Rechneigrabenstrasse

Trams
13, 15, 16
(Rechneigrabenstrasse)

The Freedom Fountain, in Late Baroque style, was set up in the
old Hühnermarkt (Poultry Market; now occupied by the
Technical Town Hall; see entry), replacing an earlier well of
1356. The name is based on a misunderstanding of an old
place-name which was interpreted as meaning an area of
sanctuary beyond the reach of the law. The Rococo statue by
Datzerath, a figure carrying his broken fetters and wearing the
cap of liberty, reflects this misunderstanding. In 1895 the
fountain was moved to the little Roseneck-Platz, which was
destroyed in 1944. It now stands in Rechneigrabenstrasse,
concealed behind office buildings.

Fressgass (officially Grosse Bockenheimer Strasse)   J16 (B24)

Location
Grosse Bockenheimer
Strasse

Grosse Bockenheimer Strasse and Kalbächer Gasse, which run
from the Opernplatz to Rathenauplatz, became known as
Fressgass (Guzzling Street) after the First World War because
of the numerous food and delicatessen shops in these streets.

In 1975–76 the Fressgass was made a pedestrian precinct.

Trams
12, 17, 21, 22
(Goetheplatz/Opernplatz)

Friedberg Gardens (Friedberger Anlage)

See Wallanlagen

Friedberger Warte

This old watch-tower with its outwork was built on the road to Friedberg in 1478, within Frankfurt's outer defensive system. After being destroyed by fire in 1634 it was rebuilt in 1637. The tower and its subsidiary buildings are now a cider bar.

Location
Friedberger Landstrasse 360

U-Bahn
U 4 to Bornheim-Mitte, then bus 34

Friedensbrücke

See Peace Bridge

Galluswarte   K14

The Galluswarte, on the west side of the town, is the oldest of four Late Gothic watch-towers which formed part of Frankfurt's outer defensive system. Built in 1414, it replaced an earlier timber tower of 1396. It was destroyed by fire in 1552 but was then rebuilt. A house and other accommodation built on to the tower in 1830 have since been demolished.

Location
Mainzer Landstrasse

S-Bahn
S 3–6 (Galluswarte)

Trams
10, 12, 14 (Galluswarte)

German Film Museum (Deutsches Filmmuseum)   K16 (D24)

Adjoining the German Museum of Architecture (see entry) is the new German Film Museum, housed in accommodation created especially for it (architects Bofinger & Partner) in a block of flats in neo-classical style dating from about 1910. In addition to the exhibition areas the building contains the Communal Cinema (Kommunales Kino) and the library of the German Film Museum and German Film Institute.

Location
Schaumainkai 41

Buses
46, 961 963, 972, 973
(Untermainbrücke)

*German Leather Museum (Deutsches Ledermuseum), Offenbach   K22

The German Leather Museum was founded in 1917 as a collection of specimens and models by the architect Hugo Eberhardt (1874–1959), who had acquired the first items in the collection in 1912. Housed from 1912 in the Villa Mainpfalz in Offenbach, it was moved in 1936 to an old warehouse (1828) used in connection with the Offenbach Fair. After adaptations to the building carried out by the founder the new museum was

Location
Frankfurter Strasse 86,
D-6050 Offenbach (just
SE of Frankfurt)

S-Bahn
S 8 (Offenbach
Hauptbahnhof)

The German Leather Museum, Offenbach

Tram
16 (Ludwigstrasse)

Opening times
Daily from 10 a.m.–5 p.m.

opened in 1938. Further rebuilding and extension became necessary in 1961 and again in 1980–81.

The museum illustrates the artistic and fashion use of leather from prehistoric times to the present day. Combined with the German Shoe Museum (1951), it forms the largest specialised museum of its kind.

The exhibits display the processing of leather (model tannery), and craft of leatherworking (book bindings, a medieval "love casket") and the development of the leatherware industry in the 19th c. (the history of luggage), as well as material of folk interest (belts worn with traditional costume, medieval horseman's garb) and an ethnographical collection of items from all over the world.

Of particular interest are the collection of shadow shows and the large Red Indian collection (*c.* 1830).

German Museum of Architecture
(Deutsches Architekturmuseum)　　　　　　　　　　**K16 (D24)**

Location
Schaumainkai 43

Buses
46, 961, 963, 972, 973
(Untermainbrücke)

The new German Museum of Architecture is housed in a neo-classical villa dating from the first decade of the 20th c. adapted for its new function by Professor O. M. Unger. It is designed to show the interweaving of the social and ecological requirements of building with the possibilities offered by building technology and the creative intentions of the architect. Associated with the museum is a library containing publications on the history of architecture from about 1900, a collection of photographs and slides and a video collection with material relating to the architecture of the present day.

*Goethe House (Goethe-Haus)   J16 (B/C24)

The house in which Goethe was born is a typical example of the life style of well-to-do citizens of Frankfurt in the Late Baroque period. Completely destroyed during the Second World War, it was rebuilt in its original form between 1946 and 1951.

The Grosser Hirschgraben marks the position of the dry moat (*graben*) surrounding the Staufen walls, which was at one time used as an enclosure for deer (*hirsch*) and was filled in in the 16th c. There is evidence of building on the site since at least 1584. In 1733 Goethe's grandmother Cornelia acquired two adjoining half-timbered houses, in which she lived along with her son Johann Kaspar Goethe (Goethe's father) and his family. After her death in 1754 the rather cramped houses were rebuilt by a master builder named Johann Ulrich Springer, advised by Johann Friedrich von Uffenbach, who had worked as an engineer on the Old Bridge (see entry). After Goethe's departure for Weimar (1775) and the death of her husband (1782) Goethe's mother (Frau Rat Goethe, known in the family as Frau Aja) sold the house with its furniture and furnishings (1795). Subsequently the house was used for industrial purposes. In 1863, however, it was acquired by Dr Otto Volger and the Freies Deutsches Hochstift (Free German Foundation) which he had helped to establish, and was thus preserved and restored to its former condition.

Although the present contents of the house are of the right period, very few of the items on display actually belonged to the Goethe family.

Location
Grosser Hirschgraben 23

U–Bahn
U 1–3 (Hauptwache)

S–Bahn
S 1–6, S 14 (Hauptwache)

Trams
17, 21, 22 (Goetheplatz)

Opening times
Mon.–Sat. 9 a.m.–6 p.m.,
Sun. 10 a.m.–1 p.m.

*Goethe Museum   J16 (B/C24)

The Goethe Museum, directly linked with the Goethe House (see entry), displays documents and other material relating to Goethe's life and activities which give a picture of his poetic world and personal development. The exhibits are arranged in the museum's 14 rooms under a number of different headings:
Paintings of the story of Joseph by Johann George Trautmann
Paintings and busts of the contemporaries of Goethe's earlier years
Goethe's Weimar circle
Goethe's Italian journey
Classical antiquity
Portraits of Goethe
View of Thuringia (the region in which Weimar lies) in Goethe's time
Goethe's later years
Goethe and the Romantic movement
View of Germany in Goethe's time

Location
Grosser Hirschgraben 23–25

U–Bahn
U 1–4 (Hauptwache)

S–Bahn
S 1–6, S 14 (Hauptwache)

Trams
17, 21, 22 (Goetheplatz)

Opening times
Mon.–Sat. 9 a.m.–6 p.m.,
Sun. 10 a.m.–1 p.m.

In addition to the Goethe House and the Goethe Museum the Freies Deutsches Hochstift also maintains the Goethe Library, with some 125,000 volumes of primary and secondary material on German literature from about 1750 to 1850. Having given up the original idea of establishing a fully comprehensive library, the foundation has concentrated since 1885 on the pre-classical period, Goethe and his circle, and the Romantic period. There is also a manuscript collection, with more than 30,000 autograph documents.

Goethe Library

Goethe House

Birthplace of Johann Wolfgang von Goethe
(b. 28 August 1749, d. 22 March 1832 in Weimar)

House of the Three Lyres
(Zu den drei Leiern)
Grosser Hirschgraben 23

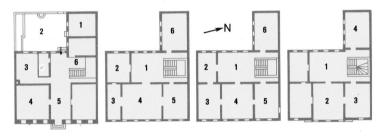

GROUND FLOOR (Baroque)	FIRST FLOOR (Rococo)	SECOND FLOOR (Louis XVI)	THIRD FLOOR (Louis XVI)
1 Garden Room	1 Hall (two cupboards)	1 Hall (astronomical clock)	1 Hall
2 Yard	2 Chimney Room (closed)	2 Birth Room	2 Poets' Room
3 Kitchen	3 South Room	3 Frau Rat's Room	3 Side Room (Puppet Theatre
4 Dining Room (Blue Room)	4 Middle Room (''Pekin'')	4 Picture Room	Room)
5 Hall	5 North Room	5 Father's Library	4 Museum Room (views of
6 Staircase Hall	6 Music Room	6 Cornelia's Room	Frankfurt in Goethe's time)

Adjoining the Goethe House to the north are the *Goethe Library* and the **Goethe Museum**. The Museum depicts Goethe's life from his departure for Weimar (1775) to his death – a ''biography in pictures''.

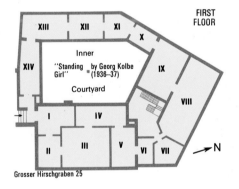

FIRST FLOOR

Grosser Hirschgraben 25

Goethe Museum

I   Frankfurt artists of Goethe's early years
II   Contemporaries of the young Goethe
III   Paintings by A. Graff and J. H. Füssli
IV   Goethe's circle in Weimar
V   Goethe's Italian journey
VI   Angelika Kauffmann
VII   Cast of Ludovisi Juno
      Views of Rome by Piranesi
VIII Italian landscapes by J. P. Hackert
IX   Portraits of the aging Goethe
X   Views of Thuringia
XI   Goethe's later years
XII   Romantic period (C. D. Friedrich, etc.)
XIII C. Brentano, A. von Arnim
XIV German landscapes and towns

Goethe Tower (Goetheturm)   M19

Location
Sachsenhäuser
Landwehrweg

Buses
36, 960 (Hainer Weg)

On the eastern fringe of the Stadtwald (see entry), above the Mühlberg Gardens, there stood in the 19th c. an outlook tower erected by the local amenity association. The Goethe Tower, the highest timber tower in Germany (43 m (141 ft)), was built in 1931, using 171 cu. m (6040 cu. ft) of timber from the Stadtwald. From the top of the tower there are superb panoramic views of Frankfurt and the surrounding area. Close by are the Goetheturm and Scheerwald play parks for children.

Grossmarkthalle

See Central Market Hall.

* Grüneburg Park and Schönhof Pavilion — G/H15

The area which is now the Grüneburg Park was occupied in the
14th c. by the Grüneburg, a fortified manor which was rebuilt
between 1789 and 1837 in accordance with the ideas of its
new owner, Bethmann-Metzler. From 1837 onwards, under
the ownership of Amschel Meyer Rothschild, the park was
landscaped in the English manner; then between 1880 and
1903 it was given its present form by Heinrich Siesmayer und
Veit.

U-Bahn
U 1–3 (Holzhausenstrasse)

Bus
36 (Grüneburgweg)

In 1964 a garden pavilion, an octagonal building in neo-
classical style which had been built for Karl-Ludwig von
Barckhaus-Wiesenhütten at Schönhof in Bockenheim, was
taken down and re-erected in the Grüneburg Park. The
pavilion, originally built at the end of the 18th c., was burned
down in 1819 and subsequently restored, probably by
Friedrich Rumpf (who may have followed the ideas of the
French architect Salins de Montfort).
Opposite the pavilion is a charming little porter's lodge (by
Franz von Hoven, *c.* 1875).
At the south-east corner of the park is the I.G. Farben Building
(see entry).

Schönhof Pavilion

Gutenberg Monument (Gutenberg-Denkmal) — J16 (B24)

A model of this monument, designed by Eduard Schmidt von
der Launitz, was displayed on the 400th anniversary of the
invention of printing in 1840, but the monument itself was
executed only between 1854 and 1858. On its Gothic-style
sandstone base are three colossal figures of Gutenberg, Fust
and Schöffer; round the base runs a frieze of famous printers,
publishers and booksellers, and at the four corners are
allegorical figures of Theology, Poetry, Science and Industry. In
niches below are the coats of arms of Mainz, Strassburg,
Frankfurt and Venice, the four towns where printing was first
practised.
The monument was temporarily removed during the replanning
of the Rossmarkt, Goetheplatz and Rathenauplatz area.

Location
Rossmarkt

U-Bahn
U 1–3 (Hauptwache)

S-Bahn
S 1–6, S 14 (Hauptwache)

Trams
17, 21, 22
(Hauptwache/Rossmarkt)

* Hauptwache (Main Guard-House) — J16 (B24/25)

Now a busy interchange point on the S-Bahn and U-Bahn, the
square known as An der Hauptwache was important in the
17th c. for the control of traffic in the Zeil and the Rossmarkt
and on the important main road to the Eschenheim Tower (see
entry). A guard-house was built by the municipal authorities in
1671, but by 1728 this was in such a dilapidated state that it
had to be replaced by a new one.
The new guard-house, designed by the Municipal Architect,

U-Bahn
U 1–3 (Hauptwache)

S-Bahn
S 1–6, S 14 (Hauptwache)

Trams
17, 21, 22 (Goetheplatz)
12 (Schillerstrasse/Börse)

The Hauptwache, now the central feature of a pedestrian precinct

Johann Jakob Samheimer, and erected in the Paradeplatz in 1729–30, was a single-storey rectangular building, with imposing pillared arcades on the front facing the Katharinenkirche (see entry). Above the three central arches was a shallow pediment carved by Johann Bernhard Schwarzenberger with the municipal coat of arms flanked by flags and weapons. Behind the mansard windows were cells for minor delinquents, in the vaulted basement cells for those guilty of more serious crimes. On the side facing the square was an area enclosed by bollards and iron chains and containing two cannon.

A commemorative tablet recalls the occasion on Good Friday 1833 when an unsuccessful attempt was made by a group of revolutionaries belonging to the Constitutional Movement, the Fatherland Union and the Burschenschaften (student organisations) to storm the guard-house and thus give the signal for a German revolution.

The Hauptwache has been a café since 1904. It was last renovated in 1981–82.

Hauptwache Fountain

Behind the Hauptwache is the Hauptwache Fountain (Hauptwache-Brunnen), a neo-classical fountain erected about 1800 to replace a Renaissance well, known as the Golden Well because of its gilded balls borne on obelisks.

To the north of the Hauptwache is the terraced access to the Hauptwache S-Bahn and U-Bahn station, on Level B of which is a pedestrian zone with numerous shops and information bureaux extending underground as far as Rathenauplatz.

Heilig-Geist-Hospital (Hospital of the Holy Ghost)

See Wallanlagen

Heilig-Geist-Kirche (Church of the Holy Ghost)

See Dominican Friary

Heimchen Housing Estate (Siedlung Heimchen), Höchst

In 1890 Wilhelm Meister, one of the founders of the Hoechst
dyestuffs firm, set aside money to build houses for workers and
foremen of the firm near their place of work. The houses were
to be let rent-free for life. Accordingly from 1891 onwards there
grew up in the south-west of Unterliederbach, an outlying
district of Frankfurt, the complex called the Arbeiterheim
(Workers' Home), popularly known as Heimchen (Little
Home).
One of the houses in the scheme won a prize at the Paris
Exhibition of 1900.

Location
Höchst-Unterliederbach

S-Bahn
S 1–3 (Höchst)

Buses
50, 57, 58
(Peter-Bied-Strasse)

Hellerhof Housing Estate (Hellerhofsiedlung)   K12/13

The Hellerhof estate, in the Gallus district to the north of the
Frankenallee, was built by the Hellerhof housing company
between 1929 and 1931 to the plans of the Dutch architect
Mart Stam. The scheme – part of Ernst May's plan for the
development of Frankfurt – is a striking example of the
functional architecture of the Neue Sachlichkeit (New
Objectivity) school promoted by the Bauhaus, which had been
founded in 1926, and at the same time exemplifies German
housing policy of the period after the First World War, designed
to produce dwellings with the lowest possible rent but without
sacrificing essential housing standards. The estate comprised
800 houses, each with a balcony and with a built-in kitchen
and bathroom; heating was provided by a district heating
scheme. The buildings on the periphery, with shops on the
south side, were deliberately kept lower in order to avoid
overshadowing the gardens within the estate.
Some of the houses (Frankenallee 176–182) were restored in
1979–80. In 1976 the block at Frankenallee 202–218 was
demolished, in spite of numerous protests, and replaced by
houses for old people. The Peace Church (Friedenskirche),
built in 1925, is a notable example of modern architecture,
showing the influence of Expressionism.

Location
Frankenallee

Trams
10, 12, 14
(Rebstöcker Strasse)

Henninger Tower (Henninger-Turm)   L17

The Henninger Tower on the Sachsenhäuser Berg was built in
1959–61 as a silo for the storage of barley for the Henninger
Brewery. There are extensive views over Frankfurt from its two
restaurants with revolving platforms and from the small
Brewing Museum above the silo, all reached by express lifts
(charge). The Frankfurter Salon, Offenbacher Salon and roof-
garden restaurant can also be reached by climbing 731 steps.
The tower is the highest viewpoint on the south bank of the
Main (120 m (395 ft)).

Location
Hainer Weg 60–64

Buses
960, 961, 963, 972, 973
(Brauerei)

Hessen Radio (Hessischer Rundfunk)   F/G16

Location
Bertramstrasse 8

U-Bahn
U 1–3
(Miquelallee/Adickesallee)

Buses
32, 33 (Bertramstrasse)

The radio and television studios and offices of Hessen Radio are in Bertramstrasse.

The building, previously occupied by a teachers' training college, was altered in 1949 (architect Gerhard Weber) and a new circular building was added. It was then designed for the use of the Bundestag; but when the choice of a federal capital fell on Bonn it was handed over to Hessen Radio. The seating in the main chamber, already partially completed, was torn out and replaced by normal floors with studios and offices.

Within the grounds is the old watch-tower of the Kühhornhof (14th c.), part of Frankfurt's medieval defences.

Hessian Monument (Hessendenkmal)

See Wallanlagen

*High-rise office blocks (Hochhäuser)   City centre

Since the last war and the post-war reconstruction the old Frankfurt city centre has taken on a very different aspect. Its skyline is now dominated by the numerous high-rise office blocks of the Banking District.

The Dresdner Bank, 166 m (545 ft) high, is one of the city's tallest buildings. The Bank für Gemeinwirtschaft (Cooperative Bank) in the Theaterplatz, built in 1977, is 156 m (512 ft) high, faced with natural-coloured aluminium and reflective windows (see cover picture); in addition to the offices of the bank there are three shopping floors with elegant shops and restaurants. The Deutsche Bank in the Taunus Gardens has two pentagonal towers entirely faced with reflective glass.

The concentration of these high-rise blocks in the city centre soon earned Frankfurt the names of "Mainhattan" and "Chicago on the Main".

*Historical Garden (Historischer Garten)   J/K17 (C25)

Location
Römerberg

U-Bahn
U 4 (Römer)

The Historical Garden, situated in the angle between the Technical Town Hall (see entry) and the recently redeveloped Ostzeile (Römerberg (see entry)), is an area of excavations, begun in 1953, which have brought to light part of the Roman settlement on this site and the foundations of the royal stronghold of Carolingian times. This is the very oldest part of Frankfurt.

*Historical Museum (Historisches Museum)   K17 (C25)

Location
Saalgasse 19

The Historical Museum was founded in 1867, and in 1893 – now supported by an association formed for the purpose in

Henninger Tower – grain silo and viewpoint ▶

Höchst

U-Bahn
U 4 (Römer)

1877 – moved into the Leinwandhaus (Stone House; see entry) and other premises. Although these buildings were destroyed during the Second World War the Museum's holdings were saved.

In 1972 the Museum was reopened in the Saalhof, now restored. It occupies the eastern (Staufen) range, which includes the Saalhof chapel, together with the Burnitz and Bernus wings, the Rententurm and the barbican of the Fahrtor. A new range of buildings to the north and west (designed by F. W. Jung and R. Schanty) combines with the historic buildings to form a square surrounding an inner courtyard.

Information centre

The Museum is seen not merely as a place for preserving relics of Frankfurt's past but above all as an information centre designed to make possible a critical study and understanding of history. In order to achieve this objective new didactic methods have been brought into play; and graphic presentations, slides, films and the electronic media all make their contribution towards bringing about this "dialogue with history".

In the new building the material is displayed in chronological order.

Ground floor: 20th c. (with periodic special exhibitions); Children's Museum; information; cafeteria.

First floor: 19th c.; Library; Coin Cabinet.

Second floor: 16th–18th c.; Graphic Collection.

The Coin Cabinet contains a large collection of German coins. The Graphic Collection includes material illustrating the development of the city.

The old buildings contain material which it is not possible to display in the new building. Most of it is in store-rooms where it can seen by visitors.

Basement: documentation on excavations in Frankfurt old town, with objects recovered.

Ground floor: stone sculpture and architectural fragments from old Frankfurt buildings now demolished; model of the old town.

First floor: 18th c. and earlier periods; dometic material of Staufen times.

Second floor: 18th–20th c.; costume collection.

Communication centre

The Museum is designed not only to give an understanding of history but also to serve as a communication centre. On the ground floor, therefore, there is a hall of some size for lectures and film shows. Here, too, is the Communal Cinema (Practical Information, Cinemas (see entry)).

Periodic special exhibitions are put on by the Historical Museum in the Rothschildpalais (see entry).

---

*Höchst   K/L6/7

Location
10 km (6 miles) W of
Frankfurt city centre

S-Bahn
S 1, S 2 (Höchst)

Höchst, well known as a centre of the chemical industry, is situated on the Main some 10 km (6 miles) west of Frankfurt city centre. It was incorporated in the city in 1928.

In Roman times there was a trading settlement at the junction of the Nidda with the Main, and in the time of Augustus this was given the protection of a fort built on the steep river-bank where St Justin's Church now stands (until about A.D. 260). On the opposite bank of the Nidda was a large military brick-

Excavations in the Historical Garden

Baroque sculpture in the Historical Museum

Höchst: Old Town

. . . and Main Gate

making establishment. The place first appears in the records in 790 under the name of Hostat. The Church of St Justin was founded in Carolingian times. The Emperor Charles IV gave Höchst its municipal charter in 1355, and in 1368 the right to levy tolls. During this period the town was used by the Bishops of Mainz as a base against the free Imperial city of Frankfurt. In 1622, during the Thirty Years War, the town and the castle (Schloss Höchst) were taken by storm and plundered by Duke Christian of Brunswick.

During the 18th c. the first industries began to be established in a new town founded in 1768 by the Elector of Mainz, Emmerich Josef von Breidbach-Bürresheim. A plan providing for a regular grid layout, with four churches for different denominations, was prepared by a Lieutenant of Grenadiers, Johann Jakob Schneider, but only a small part of this was ever carried out. Between 1772 and 1774 a factory and mansion (the Bolongaropalast) were built for the Bolongaro family of snuff-manufacturers.

A porcelain manufactory was established in Höchst in 1746 and operated until 1796; it was re-established in 1947 and now occupies the Dalberghaus (restored 1977). In 1863 the dyestuffs firm Farbwerke Meister, Lucius & Brüning was founded – now, under the name of Hoechst, the town's largest industrial establishment.

Fortifications

Of Höchst's earliest fortifications, dating from the Staufen period, there remains some fragments of walls, constructed of large rusticated blocks, in the banks of the Main to the west of the Batterie. Towards the end of the 12th c. the village of Höchst passed to the Archbishop of Mainz, and thereafter marked the archbishopric's eastern boundary with the territory of Frankfurt. In 1355 Archbishop Gerlach I secured a municipal charter for Höchst, and at the beginning of the following year the Emperor Charles IV granted the town the right to build walls, hold markets and dispense justice. The fortifications which were then built, comprising a circuit of walls with a wall-walk, 11 towers and gates and a moat, enclosed a roughly rectangular area opposite the site of the old village on both sides of the main road (now Bolongarostrasse), extending farther towards the north. In the 15th c. Diether von Isenburg strengthened the fortifications along the river in solid and handsome masonry, as can be seen in the Batterie, built of heavy blocks of sandstone, with a wall-walk and repeated representations of the coat of arms of Mainz surmounting Late Gothic tracery.

The entrance to the town on the side facing the Main was through the Main Gate (Maintor) in the Late Gothic wall of the outer ward, which bears the Isenburg coat of arms and marks indicating high water levels. The outer ward was built by Diether von Isenburg to provide additional protection for the Toll Tower (Zollturm; c. 1355–60, with half-timbering of 1664).

The view of the river, with the castle, the towers of the old town walls and St Justin's Church, is one of the most attractive in Hessen. It is best seen from the left bank of the Main (which can be crossed by ferry).

Between the Main and Bolongarostrasse is the Schlossplatz, surrounded by picturesque houses painted in a uniform colour scheme. To the south-west of the square, linked with it by a bridge over the old moat, stands Schloss Höchst.

Castle (Schloss Höchst)

In 1356 Archbishop Gerlach of Mainz began the construction of a castle designed to enforce the collection of tolls – disregarding the fact that Frederick Barbarossa had abolished all tolls on the Main in 1156 in an effort to encourage trade. The castle, 65 m (213 ft) square, with an inner courtyard and a 20 m (65 ft) wide moat, was probably built on the remains of an earlier structure of the Romanesque period. The levying of tolls at Höchst hampered the trade of the Frankfurt Fair, and accordingly the men of Frankfurt burned the castle down in 1397. Rebuilding was halted in 1408 by an Imperial Edict and was resumed only in the time of Diether von Isenburg. Between 1586 and 1608 Elector Wolfgang von Dalberg built a Renaissance castle on the same site, but this was burned down in 1635 by the troops of Duke Bernhard of Weimar. Of this building, which originally consisted of four wings, only the north-eastern part survived.

In 1665 the moat was drained and a beginning was made with the restoration of the remains. In 1681 the Gothic keep was topped with a gallery, stone helm roof and lantern. The block containing living quarters, with its curved gables, dates from the end of the 16th c., as does the lavishly conceived gatehouse. The round tower at one corner was built about 1400.

In the schloss is the Museum of the History of Höchst (opened 1975), with prehistoric and Roman material and documents on the history of the town. On the ground floor is the house museum of Farbwerke Hoechst.

Museums in Schloss

Between the schloss and St Justin's Church is the Old Town

Old Town Hall

63

Höchst

Schloss Höchst

St Justin's Church

Hall, with two stepped gables topped by stone balls. It was built by a North Italian architect, Oswald Stupanus, after a fire in 1586 which did much damage in the town.

St Justin's Church

St Justin's Church (R.C.) is the oldest church within the city of Frankfurt. It is believed to have been founded in the 7th or 8th c., and a new church was probably built when the relics of St Justin were brought from Rome to Höchst in the time of Otgar of Mainz (826–847). Excavation has shown this church to have been an aisled basilica on a T-shaped plan with three apses. By 1090, when it was made over to the Benedictines of St Alban's in Mainz, it was already much dilapidated. In 1432 it became the parish church, and thereafter was given its present form by the Antonite friars who came to Höchst in 1441. Between 1443 and 1460 they built a lofty choir on the site of the principal apse. Originally vaulted, the choir was given a flat roof in 1523; the present vaulting dates from 1931.

Attached to the choir are three chapels adjoining the north aisle, with ribbed and reticulated vaulting. The imposing main doorway, leading into a porch with reticulated vaulting, is flanked by figures of St Paul of Thebes and St Antony the Hermit (copies: the originals are inside the church).

The Carolingian nave with its column-borne arches – notable particularly for their beautiful leaf-capitals and imposts – was left intact in the rebuilding of the church.

Antonite Friary

In Bolongarostrasse (Nos. 139 and 143) are remains of the Antonite Friary of Höchst, the largest house of this secular order in Germany. The Late Gothic conventual buildings were much altered from the 16th c. onwards; a few remains are still preserved in a two-storey oriel of 1586 and a stucco ceiling (probably by Georg Hennicke, *c.* 1739) on the upper floor. Most of the buildings were demolished in 1809–11; the north wing with its Late Gothic gable survived.

Opposite the remains of the Antonite Friary is the Cronberger Haus, a stone-built house erected in 1577–80 for Franz von Cronberg and subsequently much altered. Its present aspect dates from the 19th c., when it housed the Town Hall and a school.

Cronberger Haus

Farther west Bolongarostrasse joins the Wed, in which is the town house of the Greiffenclau family, who belonged to the nobility of Mainz. To the rear of the house are the domestic offices, and in the angle of the old town walls is an octagonal tower.

Almost half of the town was destroyed by a great fire in 1586. Among the handsomest of the half-timbered buildings which survived the fire is the Gasthaus zum Anker or Anchor Inn. Above its vaulted cellars and massive ground floor are two projecting upper storeys of identical half-timbered structure, in a style transitional between the Middle Ages and the Renaissance. The inn was destroyed by fire in 1973 but was rebuilt in its original form in 1975–76, using surviving fragments of the structure.

Gasthaus zum Anker (Anchor Inn)

At the west end of Bolongarostrasse, just inside the town walls adjoining the old Lower Gate (Untertor) is the Dalberghaus, with a vaulted cellar, a ground and first floor in solid masonry and a half-timbered top floor under a high hipped roof. The house was built in 1582 for Hartmut von Cronberg, an important Mainz official, sold to Archbishop Wolfgang von Dalberg in 1586 and rebuilt immediately after the great fire in December of that year. It is now occupied by the new porcelain manufactory of Höchst.

Dalberghaus

This – the third porcelain manufactory to be established in Europe, after Dresden (1711) and Vienna (1719) – was founded in 1746, and continued in existence, with short interruptions and under different managements, until 1796. After 150 years of inactivity it was re-established in 1965.
Some new designs are produced, but the main output of the manufactory consists of reproductions of 18th c. originals, the most popular being those of Laurentius Russinger (1753–67) and his successor Johann Peter Melchior (1768–79).

Porcelain manufactory

The Bolongaropalast, a monumental complex which now belongs to the town of Höchst and is occupied by the district administration, is situated above the junction of the Nidda with the Main, on what is probably the most beautiful site in the Emmerichstadt district. It was built in 1772–74 by the snuff-manufacturers Josef Maria Markus Bolongaro (d. 1779) and his brother Jakob Philipp (d. 1780), who came from Stresa on Lake Maggiore. This Baroque palace has three wings and a street front 117 m (384 ft) long, relieved by a projecting central block. In the garden, laid out in two terraces overlooking the Main, are two pavilions with double mansard roofs, the more westerly of which was built as a residence for the Archbishop of Mainz and is now occupied by the municipal registry office. Notable features of the main palace are the chapel and a series of rooms with rich stucco decoration, centred on a reception

Bolongaropalast (Bolongaro Palace)

Bolongaropalast

room with walls decorated in early neo-classical style and a vaulted ceiling.

To the west of the Bolongaropalast, extending along Kranengasse, is the old snuff factory, a three-storey building erected at the same time as the palace (which housed the firm's offices as well as the owners' residence) but in a simpler style. After the death of the Bolongaro brothers and Archbishop Emmerich Josef of Mainz, patron of the Bolongaros, the factory was wound up (1785). The Bolongaropalast was acquired by the town in 1908, with the help of Gustav von Brüning, for use as a town hall; the district administration moved into the building in 1928.

St Joseph's Church

In Hostatostrasse is the Parish Church (R.C.) of St Joseph (St. Josef), a neo-Romanesque aisled basilica with transepts built in 1907–08. Restoration work on the fine interior, with its Art Nouveau decoration and furnishings was completed in 1980.

Hoechst factory and offices

The area between Höchst and Sindlingen is occupied by the factory and offices of the Hoechst company. Founded in 1862 as a dyestuffs factory, the firm began to manufacture fuchsine (a magenta dye) in 1863 in a factory in the Schützenbleiche area. The rapid growth of the firm (which in 1867 adopted the style Meister, Lucius & Brüning) made it necessary to move to the present site, which offered sufficient scope for expansion into one of the largest chemical plants in the world. In addition to dyestuffs and pharmaceuticals the firm is now mainly involved in the manufacture of artificial fabrics.

The firm's new administrative offices, designed by Peter Behrens, were begun in 1920 and completed in 1924 – a year before the amalgamation of Germany's six leading chemical

The Hoechst offices . . .   *. . . and Century Hall*

manufacturers to form the I.G. Farben corporation. They consist of two four-storey ranges in clinker brick, respectively 65 m (213 ft) and 72·5 m (238 ft) long, intersecting at an angle, with the entrance hall and a projecting tower containing lifts at the point of intersection. In the triangular hall stalagmite-like pillars rise up from the floor, increasing in girth as they go up, until after the fourth floor they grow together, allowing light to enter through cupolas inserted in the roof. The effect of height is enhanced by the pattern of colour, ranging from warm colours at the bottom to cold colours at the top. In both form and quality of execution the building is one of the finest examples of Expressionist architecture.

The bridge from the staircase hall of the new building to the old offices (1893), also designed by Peter Behrens, is world-famous as the emblem of the firm.

On the road to Zeilsheim, at Pfaffenwiese 301, is the Jahr-hunderthalle (Century Hall), designed by Friedrich Wilhelm Krämer, which was built in 1961–63 to mark the firm's centenary. The thin concrete shell of the dome, 86 m (282 ft) in diameter, is borne on six columns linked by a cornice.

Jahrhunderthalle (Century Hall)

The building is designed to serve a variety of purposes, and for major events can accommodate between 2000 and 3500 people. Included in the complex are a hotel, a casino with seating for 700 and a restaurant with seating for 350.

Holy Ghost Church (Heilig-Geist-Kirche)

See Dominican Friary

Holy Ghost Hospital (Heilig-Geist-Hospital)

See Wallanlagen

Holzhausenschlösschen (Museum of Prehistory and Early History)   H16

Location
Justinianstrasse 5

Bus
36 (Hynspergstrasse)

Opening times
Tue.–Sun. 10 a.m.–5 p.m.,
Wed. 10 a.m.–8 p.m.

The Holzhausenschlösschen, a Baroque palace surrounded by a moat, lies in Holzhausen Park at the end of an avenue of chestnut trees, at the entrance to which from the Oeder Weg there was formerly a neo-classical gateway. It was originally one of the fortified manor houses of the Frankfurt nobility within the protection of the town's defensive system which were later used as country residences.

The property of Oede, which first appears in the records in 1398, was acquired in 1503 by Hamman von Holzhausen. In 1540 Justinian von Holzhausen enlarged the house into a country mansion, which was burned down only 12 years later during the War of the League of Schmalkalden. It was subsequently rebuilt and survived the Thirty Years War unscathed. In 1722 Louis Rémy de la Fosse, who as Architect to the Landgrave of Hessen had designed his palace in Darmstadt, was commissioned by Johann Hieronymus von Holzhausen, who had just become Junior Burgomaster of Frankfurt, to rebuild the house. Begun in 1726 and completed in 1729, the new house was transformed from a fortified manor house into a palatial country residence. In 1910 the last of the

The Holzhausenschlösschen

The monumental I.G. Farben offices

Holzhausens transferred his estate to a property development company, and the land round the park became a select residential district.

Since 1953 the Holzhausenschlösschen has been occupied by the Museum of Prehistory and Early History (Museum für Vor- und Frühgeschichte), which has a collection of material from Neolithic to medieval times, including finds from recent excavations in Frankfurt old town (Historical Museum (see entry)). Finds from the Roman settlement of Nida are displayed in the Deutschordenshaus (see entry).

Museum of Prehistory and Early History

I.G. Farben Offices   H15/16

The I.G. Farben offices, originally planned as the headquarters of the Hoechst concern, were designed by Hans Poelzig, winner of an architectural competition, and built in 1928–30. They occupy the site of an establishment for epileptics and the insane of which Heinrich Hoffmann (author of the famous children's book "Struwwelpeter") was Director. The building, faced with travertine, is a magnificent example of functional architecture and of the successful accommodation of a large building into a park-like landscape. The grounds were laid out by Max Bromme. In 1945 General Eisenhower chose the I.G. Farben offices as the United States Headquarters in Germany. In 1955 it became the property of the Federal Government but is still in American occupation (Headquarters of the Fifth Army Corps, offices of various U.S. agencies).

Location
Grüneburgplatz

U-Bahn
U 1–3 (Holzhausenstrasse)

Bus
36 (Simon-Bolivar-Anlage)

Iron Bridge, now for pedestrians only

Iron Bridge (Eiserner Steg)   K16/17 (C25)

U-Bahn
U 4 (Römer)

Bus
46 (Sachsenhäuser Ufer)

Boat landing-stage
"Wikinger", "Primus"

By the middle of the 19th c. the Old Bridge (see entry), the only road connection between Frankfurt town centre and Sachsenhausen, was no longer adequate for the traffic it had to bear, and a company was formed to build a new bridge at the Fahrtor. Lack of space, however, particularly on the right bank of the Main, prevented the construction of access ramps for a road bridge. Construction of an iron truss suspension bridge designed by Peter Schmick, Chief Municipal Engineer, began in 1868, and the new bridge was opened in September 1869. Until the bridge was taken over by the town at the beginning of January 1869 all users had to pay a toll of 1 kreutzer towards the amortisation of the cost of construction (120,000 florins). The bridge, 174 m (190 yd) long between the abutments of red Main sandstone, has several times been adjusted to changing navigational conditions by the raising of the roadway. It was blown up towards the end of the Second World War and subsequently reconstructed in its original form.

Jewish cemeteries   F17, G17, J17 (B26)

U-Bahn
U 5 (Eckenheimer Landstrasse)

The modern cemetery building in the Eckenheimer Landstrasse (No. 238), designed by Fritz Nathan and built in 1928–29, together with the new cemetery laid out at the same time, supplemented the older Jewish cemetery in Rat-Beil-Strasse. That cemetery, with a neo-classical gateway by Friedrich

Rumpf, was opened in 1828 and was itself the successor to the medieval Jewish cemetery in Battonnstrasse.
The oldest Jewish burial-place (1462–1828), in Batton-strasse, is near the old ghetto, which was set aside for the Jewish population of the town in 1460 and opened up only in 1811. This cemetery is unique in its unity and historical continuity. There are other Jewish burial-grounds at Heddern-heim, Nied, Niederursel (see entry), Höchst (see entry), Bockenheim and Rödelheim.

Bus
45 (Rat-Beil-Strasse)

Justice Fountain (Gerechtigkeitsbrunnen)   K16 (C25)

The Justice Fountain was set up in 1541–43 in the time of Benedikt Loscher, Municipal Architect – probably on the site of an earlier well. The water was brought from the Friedberger Feld, to the north of the town, in a pipe 2 km (1¼ miles) long. The fountain was renovated in 1594, and in 1610 Johann Kocheisen or Hocheisen added a figure of Justice on a stone base. On 14 June 1614, on the occasion of the Coronation of the Emperor Matthias, the fountain was fitted with an eagle's head and a lion's head which dispensed white and red wine: an experiment which was not repeated in view of the waste which it involved. In 1805 the fountain was again renovated for the Emperor Francis I of Austria, but thereafter it fell into a state of dilapidation. Finally in 1887, at the expense of a wine-dealer named G. D. Manskopf, Kocheisen's stone figure of Justice, together with the associated Sirens and the reliefs of Virtues (Caritas, Spes, Temperantia, Justitia), was copied by Friedrich Schierhold, a teacher at the Academy, and cast in bronze in Nuremberg. The wrought-iron railings (also 1887) were the work of Alexander Linnemann.

Location
Römerberg

U-Bahn
U 4 (Römer)

Trams
13, 14, 15, 16, 18
(Paulskirche)

Justice Fountain

Kaiserstrasse   K15/16 (C23/24)

U-Bahn
U 4 (Hauptbahnhof)
U 1–4 (Theaterplatz)

To the east of the Central Station (see entry) extends the Bahnhofsviertel (Station District), covering an area of 22 ha (54 acres). Its logitudinal streets, aligned on the railway lines leading to the old West Stations on the Taunus Gardens, are intersected by cross streets which divide the area into blocks of roughly equal size. The streets themselves are lined with five-storey blocks of flats – handsome examples of the residential building of the Gründerzeit (the period of rapid industrial expansion in the early 1870s). The main axis of the district and its link with the city centre was the Kaiserstrasse. This tree-lined avenue, some 30 m (100 ft) wide, is notable for the high architectural quality of its offices and hotels, designed by leading Frankfurt architects of the Gründerzeit. The street intersections are enlarged into small squares by cutting off the corners and given architectural importance by domed super-structures.

The Kaiserstrasse – like the rest of the Bahnhofsviertel – is more a business than a residential district, with a concentration of travel agencies and airline offices, tobacconists, furriers and photographic shops. The side streets, named after the rivers Elbe, Weser, Mosel (Moselle), Neckar and Nidda, are the stronghold of Frankfurt's entertainment industry.

Katharinenkirche (St Catherine's Church)   J16 (B25)

Location
An der Hauptwache

U-Bahn
U 1–3 (Hauptwache)

S-Bahn
S 1–6, S 14 (Hauptwache)

Trams
17, 21, 22 (Goetheplatz)

On the south side of the square named An der Hauptwache is St Catherine's Church (Protestant), on the site of a medieval hospice founded by Magister Wicker Frosch in 1343. Of the two churches built in 1344 one – the Holy Cross Chapel – served the hospice, while the other, dedicated to SS. Catherine and Barbara, was attached to an associated foundation for the daughters of the town nobility established in 1353.

Subsequently, thanks to munificent donations, the latter chapel was enlarged and came to be known simply as St Catherine's. The first Protestant sermon in Frankfurt was preached here by Hartmann Ibach in 1522, and soon afterwards the church was closed to Catholics and the religious house became a Protestant foundation for needy gentle-women. In 1677 the building, then in a dilapidated condition and of inadequate size, was pulled down, and in the following year work began on a new church.

This new preaching church, designed by Melchior Hessler, the Municipal Engineer, had a high hipped roof and a tower in the middle of the north front. The tower, three-storeyed, is topped by a balustrade with ornamental tracery and above this, set back, an octagonal superstructure bearing a dome and lantern. The architectural details – the polygonal choir, the external buttresses, the window tracery and the ribbed timber ceiling – are Baroque in feeling but based on Gothic models. The interior was surrounded on three sides by a two-storey wooden gallery, with 83 paintings of Biblical scenes in the front panels.

The church was destroyed down to its foundations in 1944 and rebuilt between 1950 and 1954 with a much simplified interior. It contains a number of tombs, including that of the founder,

Wicker Frosch (d. 1363), with a model of the church. The new
organ, with 4400 pipes, is the largest in Frankfurt.
The principal glory of the new church is its 15 stained-glass
windows by Carl Crodel – the fourth set of stained glass in the
church's 300 years of existence.

Klingspor Museum (Offenbach)   K22

The Klingspor Museum in the Büsingpalais, opened in 1953, is
a highly instructive collection of material on the art of the book
and calligraphy in the 20th c. The basis of the collection was the
private library of Karl Klingspor (1868–1950), head of an
Offenbach type-foundry of international reputation, which was
bequeathed to the town by his heirs. The museum also includes
material left by D. Rudolf Koch (1876–1934), who worked
with Klingspor and taught at the School of Applied Art in
Offenbach, and work by calligraphers of the Leipzig school
(Rudolf Spemann) and Stuttgart school (Ernst Schneidler).

Location
Herrnstrasse 80,
D-6050 Offenbach

Tram
16 (Kaiserstrasse)

Opening times
Daily 10 a.m.–5 p.m.
closed Sat. 1–2 p.m.

Kuhhirtenturm (Cowherd's Tower)   K17 (C26)

In Grosse Rittergasse in Alt-Sachsenhausen (see entry) is the
Kuhhirtenturm, the last survivor of five watch-towers in
Sachsenhausen, part of the town's defensive system, which
were still standing in 1870. The last of the five was saved from
demolition in 1884 only by the protests of the townspeople. It
is a four-storey rectangular tower built about 1490, with a half-
timbered top storey. From 1923 to 1927 it was occupied by
Paul Hindemith (1896–1963), then Director of the Frankfurt
Opera House. Adjoining the tower is a well-known cider bar of
the same name.

Location
Grosse Rittergasse

Bus
46 (Frankensteiner Platz)

Trams
11, 16
(Frankensteiner Platz)

Leather Museum

See German Leather Museum

Leinwandhaus

See Stone House

Liebfrauenberg   J17 (B25)

The Square in which the Liebfrauenkirche stands – the only
square of any size in Frankfurt old town apart from the
Römerberg – took its name from the church, becoming known
as Unserer Frauen Plan (Our Lady's Square) or the Frauenberg.
From the end of the 13th c. a horse market was held here, from
1490 a cattle market. In 1486 the citizens of Frankfurt paid
homage to the Emperor Maximilian I on the Liebfrauenberg,
and thereafter it began to take over some of the functions which
had traditionally fallen to the Römerberg. During the 16th c. the

U-Bahn
U 1–3 (Hauptwache)

S-Bahn ·
S 1–6, S 14 (Hauptwache)

municipal council sought to transfer part of the Frankfurt Fair to this site, but without success, and in 1573 the booths which had been set up for the fair were pulled down.

Fountain

Between 1594 and 1610 a fountain was erected in the square, replacing an earlier well of 1494. The fountain basin was surrounded by a balustrade decorated with coats of arms and marine creatures, and in the centre, topping the plinth with the pipes which dispensed water, was an allegorical figure. By 1769, however, the original fountain was in poor condition and had to be demolished. In the following year work began on a new fountain, under the direction of the Municipal Architect, Johann Andreas Liebhardt. The stonemason responsible was Bernhard Scheidel; the figures and sculptured ornament were the work of Johann Michael Datzerath; and the bell-founders Johann Georg and Johannes Schneidewind cast and gilded two tablets with inscriptions. The fountain was then painted – the obelisk in red, the figures, reliefs and basin in white – and was finally completed in 1771.

In the centre of the oval basin with its curving balustrade is a rusticated obelisk borne on a conical base. On either side, beside the tablets with inscriptions, are river gods pouring water into shells supported by dolphins, from whose mouths the water flows into the basin. Above the bronze tablets, flanking a carving of Frankfurt's heraldic eagle, are putti, symbolising the town's obligation to protect its citizens. The obelisk is topped by a gilded sun.

---

*Liebfrauenkirche (Church of Our Lady) J17 (B25)

Location
Liebfrauenberg

U-Bahn
U 1–3 (Hauptwache)

S-Bahn
S 1–6, S 14 (Hauptwache)

Tram
17 (Hauptwache)

On the Liebfrauenberg, half-way between the Zeil and Paulsplatz, stands the Liebfrauenkirche, rebuilt in 1954 after suffering destruction during the Second World War.

About 1310 Wigel von Wanebach founded a Lady Chapel just inside the Staufen walls (see entry), and this was built between 1318 and 1321 with financial assistance from his son-in-law Wicker Frosch. Subsequently it became a collegiate church and was enlarged into a Gothic hall-church. About 1430 the aisled sacristy between the choir and the walls was completed and work began, probably under the direction of Madern Ger-thener, on the south side of the church, which was to be the main front. The Three Kings Doorway, which was concealed by shops during the 16th c., was given a porch (by Friedrich Rumpf) in 1824. In the tympanum of the doorway, framed in rich tracery, is the Adoration of the Shepherds and the Three Kings, and in the spandrels are half-length figures of the prophets Isaiah and Jeremiah. A bell-tower (increased in height about 1770 and in 1954) was built on the Staufen walls, and at the same time the nave was lengthened. Then in 1506–09 followed the building of a new sacristy and a heightened choir designed by Jörg Östreicher (Dominican Friary (see entry)), and probably also the construction of the façade with its windowed gables overlooking the square.

Interior

Between 1763 and 1770 the interior was decorated in sumptuous Rococo style, but all this was destroyed during the war apart from the figures on the altar by Johann Jakob Juncker. In the rebuilding of the church the Late Gothic

In the Museum of Sculpture, Liebieghaus

vaulting was replaced by a flat timber roof, articulated in a fashion which recalls the original ribbed structure. On the north wall is the monument of the founder, Wigel von Wanebach, and in the porch is a fine Pietà of 1383 in the so-called "soft" Gothic style.

---

*Liebieghaus (Museum of Sculpture)   L16 (D23/24)

The Liebieghaus, originally a villa standing along in a park, was built in 1896 by a Munich architect named Romeis, taking as his model the fortified manor houses and burghers' houses of the 15th and 16th c. In spite of the variety of materials used, the façade on Steinlestrasse achieves its effect by clear articulation of the surfaces. The gallery wing was added in 1909, after the villa had been acquired by the city of Frankfurt to house a museum of sculpture; its façade shows the mingling of Baroque and Art Nouveau characteristic of Frankfurt architecture at the end of the 19th c.

Under its foundation charter the object of the Liebieghaus is "to illustrate the development of sculpture among civilised peoples in historical times by the collection of outstanding or characteristic works". The museum contains examples from Asia and Egypt, Greek and Roman antiquity, the Middle Ages, the Renaissance and the Baroque and Rococo periods. Notable items include:

"Ariadne", by Johann Heinrich Dannecker (1814).
Reliefs from the tomb of King Sahure (Egypt, *c.* 2500 B.C.).

Location
Schaumainkai 71

Buses
46, 961, 963, 972, 973
(Untermainbrücke)

Trams
11, 21, 22 (Schweizer Strasse/Gartenstrasse)

Museum of Sculpture
(Museum alter Plastik)

"High Official" (Sumer, c. 2500 B.C.).
"Saddled Horse" (China, 8th c. B.C.).
Myron's "Athena" (Roman marble of 1st c. A.D., after a Greek bronze of 5th c. B.C.).
Funerary lion from Cheironeia (4th c. B.C.).
"Bärbele von Ottenheim", head by Nicolaus Gerhaert (1463).
"Virgin and Child", by Tilman Riemenschneider (beginning of 16th c.).
Head of a king (Île de France, end of 12th c.).
"Assumption", majolica altar by Andrea della Robbia (15th c.).
"Mademoiselle Servat", by Jean-Antoine Houdon (18th c.).

Little Market Hall (Kleinmarkthalle)   J17 (B25)

Location
Hasengasse 5–7

U-Bahn
U 4 (Römer)

Trams
13, 14, 15, 16, 18
(Domstrasse)

The Little Market Hall was built in 1953–54 (architects Gottwald and Weber), replacing the first market hall to be built in Germany (1877–78), which until 1928 also served as the Central Market Hall (see entry). The Little Market Hall is of interest for its rich assortment of vegetables, fruit, meat, cheese and foreign produce. There was formerly also a temporary market and fish hall in Battonnstrasse.
Opening times Mon.–Fri. 8 a.m.–6 p.m., Sat. 8 a.m.–2 p.m.

Lohr Park (Seckbach)   E20

U-Bahn
U 4 to Seckbacher
Landstrasse, then bus 34 or 43

The Lohr Park, on the Lohrberg in the district of Seckbach (see entry), was laid out between 1924 and 1930. From here there are good views of the Main Valley, the Spessart and Taunus hills, the Wetterau, the Odenwald and the Vogelsberg. Here, too, can be seen the last vineyard in Frankfurt, the Lohrberger Hang.

Lower Main Bridge (Untermainbrücke)   K16 (C/D24)

U-Bahn
U 1–4 (Theaterplatz)

Trams
13, 14, 15, 16, 17, 18, 21, 22
(Theaterplatz)

The principal road link between the city centre on the north bank of the Main and Sachsenhausen on the south (Neue Mainzer Strasse–Schweizer Strasse) is the Lower Main Bridge, built by the engineer Peter Schmick in 1872–74.
The original bridge was borne on five arches, each 289 m (95 ft) wide. After being blown up in 1945 it was rebuilt in 1949 in a different form, as a plate girder bridge.

Main, River

Boat landing-stage
Iron Bridge (Eiserner Steg)

The Main, in earlier days a determining factor in the commerce of the free Imperial city, is now an important inland waterway for the transport of coal, oil, building materials, etc. The river, ranging in width between 100 and 200 m (110 and 220 yd), is spanned by 15 bridges; it is planned to replace the old Flösserbrücke. The canalisation of the Main was completed in 1886 with the construction of the Western Harbour. There are

Entrance gate . . .   *. . . to the Main Cemetery*

dams at Oberrad and Griesheim. The city's traffic development plan provides for the construction of two tunnels under the river – one near the slaughterhouse (Schlachthof) for the S-Bahn, the other at the Lower Main Bridge for the U-Bahn.

The original landing-place for the river boats on the Mainkai was replaced during the 19th c. by the Western Harbour and the larger Eastern Harbour (see entry), which are still linked by the old railway line along the bank of the Main. By the Iron Bridge (see entry) is the landing-stage for the White Fleet (Weisse Mainflotte), which operates round trips and excursions on the Main and the Rhine from spring to autumn; the trips to Rüdesheim and the Lorelei are particularly popular.

Main Cemetery (Hauptfriedhof)   F/G17

The Main Cemetery, the "cemetery outside the town", was opened in 1928 as a replacement for the overcrowded Petersfriedhof (see entry), which had been in use since the 15th c. The Old Gateway (Altes Portal) at the entrance (1928; designed by the Municipal Architect, Friedrich Rumpf) conceals behind its monumental Doric order the cemetery offices and mortuary.

Opposite the main entrance, occupying almost the whole width of the cemetery, is a line of arcades (also designed by Rumpf) with the burial-places of well-known Frankfurt families. In front of these is the oldest part of the cemetery (areas A to D), laid out by the Municipal Gardener, Sebastian Rinz, in the style of an English garden. The original cemetery

Location
Eckenheimer Landstrasse 190

U-Bahn
U 5 (Hauptfriedhof)

77

was doubled in size during the 19th c.; it was again extended between 1907 and 1912 to give it an area of 47 ha (116 acres), and the New Gateway (Neues Portal), with a service hall, mortuary and crematorium was built to the design of the Berlin architects Heinrich Reinhardt and Georg Süssenguth, in a style based on the architecture of the Late Roman period.

The cemetery now has an area of some 75 ha (18·5 acres). In addition to the graves of many notable figures it contains memorials for the dead of the two world wars and the victims of National Socialism.

Among those buried in the cemetery are Arthur Schopenhauer (1788–1860), the philosopher; Heinrich Hoffmann (1809–94), author of "Struwwelpeter"; the anthropologist Leo Frobenius (1873–1938); the writer Ricarda Huch (1864–1947); Carl Ferdinand Gutzkow (1811–78), spokesman of the Young Germany movement; members of the Frankfurt banking family of Bethmann; and the philosopher Theodor W. Adorno (1903–69).

Mercury Fountain (Merkurbrunnen)   J14

Location
Ludwig-Erhard-Anlage

Trams
16, 18 (Festhalle/
Messegelände)

The Mercury Fountain in the Ludwig Erhard Gardens, designed by Hugo Lederer, is associated with the name of the Frankfurt banker Anton Hahn. Hahn conceived the idea of presenting a monumental fountain to the city in 1909, but it was left to his sons to put his wishes into effect after his death. The fountain was originally erected in Rathenauplatz in 1916, but when the square was renamed after the Nazi hero Horst Wessel in 1933 it gave place to a monument to Schiller. Finally in 1954 the fountain, with its figure of the god of trade and traders, found an appropriate home at the main entrance to the Trade Fair Grounds (see entry).

Messegelände

See Trade Fair Grounds

Monte Scherbelino   O/P19/20

Location
Stadtwald

Bus
960 (Monte Scherbelino)

Monte Scherbelino – the name is mock-Italian, from German *scherbe,* "sherd, fragment" – lies to the south of Oberrad, near the motorway exit at the Offenbacher Kreuz. It is an artificial hill built up from 20 million tons of refuse deposited here between 1927 and 1968, which, after the establishment of a refuse-burning plant on the south-western outskirts of the Nordwest-stadt district, was covered with earth and landscaped. It is now a popular viewpoint and place of recreation, with barbecue facilities, a playground, a toboggan run, footpaths and a pond at the foot of the hill.

Municipal Archives (Stadtarchiv)

See Carmelite Friary

Villa Metzler, home of the Museum of Applied Arts

Museum of Applied Arts (Museum für Kunsthandwerk) K16 (C25)

At the east end of the Schaumainkai (Museumsufer; see entry), set in a park which has been preserved almost in its original state, is the Villa Metzler, which houses the Museum of Applied Arts. The museum was founded in 1877 and in 1921 was taken over by the city of Frankfurt.

The Villa Metzler, a country house in neo-classical style, was built in 1802–04 for a pharmacist named Peter Salzwedel and was subsequently acquired by the Metzler family of bankers and considerably altered by them in 1865. Its 14 rooms are now insufficient for the museum's collection of some 30,000 items from Europe and Asia; but after the completion of an extension designed by Richard Meyer & Partners of New York it will be possible to put the main substance of the collection on permanent display. It is planned to have departments devoted to Europe, the Islamic countries, East Asia, Eurasia, the art of the book and calligraphy, supplemented by travelling exhibitions and an educational section.

Since 1974 the museum has put on an exhibition of European furniture from Gothic to Art Nouveau from its own collection, and in addition it organises periodic special exhibitions, partly from its own resources and partly through loans from other institutions, in the exhibition hall of the Carmelite Friary (see entry).

Goldsmith's work: Baldingen Chalice, from Ulm (mid 16th c.); enamel disc by Godefroi de Claire from the Shrine of St Remaclus in Stavelot, Belgium (*c.* 1160).

Location
Schaumainkai 15

Bus
46 (Eiserner Steg)

Trams
11, 17, 21, 22 (Schweizer Strasse/Gartenstrasse)

Opening times
Tue., Thu.–Sun.
10 a.m.–5 p.m.
Wed. 10 a.m.–8 p.m.

Bronzes: Renaissance figures and utensils; aquamanile in the form of a cock (12th c.).

Furniture and wooden articles: European furniture from Gothic to Art Nouveau; domestic altars; clocks; lacquered furniture; mirrors, etc.

Textiles: Gothic tapestries (e.g. Tapestry of the Virgin, *c.* 1450).

Ceramics: faience; Hispano-Mauresque lustre dish (15th c.); Italian majolica; Preuning Jug, from Nuremberg (mid 16th c.); stoneware and earthenware from different parts of Germany.

Porcelain from all German and some foreign manufactories: Meissen "Temple of Honour" (centrepiece for table, by Kändler); Höchst porcelain.

Glass: German glasses; Venetian glass (16th c.); agate glass jug (Venice, *c.* 1500).

Islamic art: ceramics from Persia and Mesopotamia; Oriental carpets; knotted carpet (Cairo, 16th c.); Luristan bronzes.

East Asian art: Chinese bronzes and early ceramics; stoneware and ceramics from the T'ang to the Ming dynasty; Chinese blue and white porcelain of the 17th and 18th c.; lacquerware and jade.

Linel Collection of Typography and Calligraphy: development of writing from the 11th c.

Museum of Architecture

See German Museum of Architecture

Museum of Ethnology (Museum für Völkerkunde)　　　K16 (D25)

Location
Schaumainkai 29

Buses
46, 961, 963, 972, 973
(Eiserner Steg)

Opening times
Tue.–Sun. 10 a.m.–5 p.m.,
Wed. 10 a.m.–8 p.m.

Frankfurt's Museum of Ethnology is the most important German museum in its field after those of Berlin, Hamburg, Bremen and Stuttgart. Since the destruction of the Palais Thurn und Taxis in 1944 limitations of space make it impossible to show more than a small selection of items in periodic special exhibitions on particular themes.

Under the development plan for the Museumsufer (see entry) the museum is to be extended to provide additional exhibition space. The museum was founded in 1904 by Dr Bernhard Hagen and acquired much additional material from the 22 expeditions of Leo Frobenius, who was Director of the museum from 1934 to 1938.

Museum of Natural History

See Senckenberg Museum of Natural History

Museum of Prehistory and Early History

See Holzhausenschlösschen

Museumsufer – Schaumainkai　　　K/L16 (C/D23–25)

Bus
46 (Städel or Eiserner Steg)

The Schaumainkai, the embankment running along the south bank of the Main between the Dreikönigskirche (see entry) and the Peace Bridge (see entry), was developed in 1873–74 to the plans of Peter Schmick, simultaneously with the construction of the Lower Main Bridge (see entry).

From the vertical wall enclosing the river the lower part of the embankment, a strip between 15 m (50 ft) and 32 m (105 ft) wide laid out in gardens, runs up to the higher level, which is edged on the river side by a double row of pollarded planes. On the south side of the road, which was laid out from the mid 18th c. onwards in ornamental gardens and pleasure-grounds, are a series of large and handsome villas, mainly built at the end of the 19th c., most of which are now occupied by museums. The central feature of the Museumsufer is the Städel Art Institute (see entry), which was planned and built as a museum. Other museums are the Museum of Applied Arts (see entry), the Museum of Ethnology (see entry), the Federal Postal Museum (see entry), the Liebieghaus (see entry), the German Museum of Architecture (see entry) and the German Film Museum (see entry).

Natural History Museum

See Senckenberg Museum of Natural History

Nebbien Garden-House (Nebbiensches Gartenhaus)   J16 (A24

After the demolition of the town's fortifications from 1806 onwards parts of the area they had occupied were sold to private individuals on condition that they would be laid out in gardens. A Danish publisher named Markus Johann Nebbien who had come to Frankfurt in 1785 purchased one such plot of land behind his house, situated on the main road, and in 1815 built a modest garden-house in neo-classical style.

Location
Bockenheimer Anlage

U-Bahn
U 1–3 (Eschenheimer Tor)

Trams
12, 17, 21, 22 (Opernplatz)

Nieder-Erlenbach

The district of Nieder-Erlenbach, which first appears in the records in the late 8th c., belonged to Frankfurt from 1376 to 1866. The administration of the village was in the hands of a mayor appointed by the Frankfurt municipal council, who resided in a house (Alt-Erlenbach 27) erected by the council in 1748. The house was later occupied by the Protestant pastor.

For the protection of the village a senior official (Amtmann) was appointed, with armed support. At first he resided in the castle at Bonames (1402–04; see entry), and later in the castle in Nieder-Erlenbach itself, later known as the Glauburg (1405–1541). The Amtmann of the day had the right of use of the land attached to the castle. After Frankfurt ceased to appoint an Amtmann the castle was leased to tenants and then, in 1698, sold to Johann Hieronymus von Glauburg, who at once (1698–1701) proceeded to alter and enlarge it. At the beginning of the 19th c. the castle was again let on lease, and thereafter belonged to various private owners. In 1953 it was bought by the commune, which let it on hereditary leasehold to a private school, the Anna-Schmidt-Schule.

U-Bahn
U 2 to Kalbach, then bus 66

Glauburg

Lersnersches Schloss, Nieder-Erlenbach

Lersnersches Schloss

A property on the Erlenbach stream was acquired by the Lersner family, who came from the Limburg area. From 1729 onwards the family produced a number of Senior Burgomasters of Frankfurt, and one member of the family, Achilles August von Lersner, kept an important chronicle. His descendants built a house on the property which remained in the family until 1953. The Lersnersches Schloss (Zur Charlottenburg 3), in Baroque style, was erected in 1746 and altered in 1893. The Charlottenburg, a neo-Baroque manor house with domestic offices and outbuildings, was built in 1840. Behind the house is an English-style park. The Lersner family vault is in the cemetery (opened in 1831) in Kapersburgstrasse.

Parish church

Near the Lersnersches Schloss, at Zur Charlottenburg 1, stands the Protestant parish church, a small aisleless Late Gothic church which was remodelled in Baroque style in 1637.

Niederrad "Office Town" (Bürostadt Niederrad) M/N 12/13

Location
6 km (4 miles) SW of
Frankfurt city centre

Tram
21 (Bürostadt Niederrad/
Lyoner Strasse)

Niederrad "Office Town" lies between the Main and the Stadtwald (see entry). The area (about 485,000 sq. m (120 acres)) was set aside in 1959 for large firms seeking office accommodation near the business district of Frankfurt. Sites on the estate were to be used only for office buildings, and it was a condition that building was to be limited to five-tenths of the area of the site above ground and six-tenths below ground.
The first organisation to take up a site in the Bürostadt was the Federation of German Engineering Firms (VDMA), whose

high-rise office block (architects Meid & Romeick) was erected in 1965–67. Architecturally perhaps the most interesting building is the high-rise complex (architect Egon Eiermann) built in 1967–72 to house the German headquarters of Olivetti.

Niederursel   C/D12/13

The outlying district of Niederursel, incorporated in Frankfurt in 1910, is first mentioned in the records in 1132, but its origins date back to a settlement of the pre-Roman period. The old town centre with its half-timbered houses, mainly of the Baroque period, is well preserved in spite of the proximity of modern development (the Nordweststadt district).

U-Bahn
U 3 (Niederursel)

The division of Niederursel into two distinct parts can be dated back to the year 1436, when Henne von Ursel sold his property in two equal parts, one to the town of Frankfurt and the other to the noble family of Kronberg (later Solms). After the Thirty Years War there were continual disputes between the people of Frankfurt and the Counts of Solms-Rödelheim, who sought to make good the losses they had suffered during the war by squeezing more money out of the peasants. After long wrangling it was decided by the Supreme Court of the Empire in 1700 that the town should be divided into two, and the division was put into effect in 1714. Lots were drawn, and Frankfurt received the south-western part of Nieder-Ursel, the Solms-Rödelheim family the north-eastern part. Thereafter the town had two town halls – the Solms-Rödelheim one at Alt Niederursel 29 (1718), the Frankfurt one at Alt Niederursel 28 (1719). After the annexation by Prussia in 1866 the two parts came together again.

Town Halls

The Gustav-Adolf-Kirche (Gustavus Adolphus Church), centrally situated at Alt Niederursel 30, was built in 1927–28 (architect Martin Elsaesser), on an octagonal plan. It replaced a chapel, the St. Georgskapelle, which is first mentioned in the records in 1402; the old churchyard wall, with the gravestones built into it, was preserved.

Gustav-Adolf-Kirche

Nikolaikirche (St Nicholas's Church)   K17 (C25)

The Church of St Nicholas, patron of boatmen, was built in 1290 on the south side of the Römerberg (see entry), near the river. Situated as it was on land held by the king, the church was probably a replacement for the court chapel in the Saalhof (see entry). In 1282 it came under the control of the Cathedral Chapter, and in the 14th c. was increasingly reserved for the use of the municipal council. In the middle of the 15th c. it underwent extensive rebuilding and alteration; in 1460 the tower was increased in height, and thereafter a watchman stationed in the tower greeted vessels arriving and departing with a blast on his horn.
In 1466–67 the church was given its characteristic steeply pitched hipped roof, surrounded by a gallery with projecting platforms at the corners, the balustrade being decorated with

Location
Römerberg

U-Bahn
U 4 (Römer)

Trams
13, 14, 15, 16, 18
(Paulskirche)

tracery (by Hans von Lich). From the gallery the municipal council were able to watch the coronation ceremonies or games and jousting in the square below.

Nizza Gardens (Nizza-Anlage)   K16 (C24)

Location
Untermainkai

U-Bahn
U 1–4 (Theaterplatz)

Trams
13, 14, 15, 16, 17, 18, 21, 22
(Theaterplatz)

The Nizza Gardens, laid out between 1866 and 1875 on the site of the old winter harbour, extend for some 800 m ($\frac{1}{2}$ mile) along the Untermainkai (Lower Main Embankment) on either side of the Lower Main Bridge (see entry). The gardens were extended in 1932 and again in 1952; the Municipal Gardener who was responsible for the latter extension, Andreas Weber, is commemorated by a portrait medallion on the embankment wall. The gardens are named after the French resort of Nice (in German known as Nizza) because of their profusion of Mediterranean vegetation – ginkgo trees, lemon trees, fig trees and almond trees, laurels, etc.
The equatorial sundial (1951) was a gift from the old Heddernheim Copper Works.

Obermainanlage (Upper Main Gardens)

See Wallanlagen

Odeon

See Wallanlagen

Old Bridge (Alte Brücke)   K17 (C26)

Location
Kurt-Schumacher-Strasse/
Brückenstrasse

Buses
36, 960
(Elisabethanstrasse)

Until the construction of the Iron Bridge in 1869 (see entry) the Old Bridge, also known as the Sachsenhausen Bridge (Sachsenhäuser Brücke), was the only bridge over the Main in Frankfurt. Although the first mention of the bridge in the records is in 1222 it is a safe assumption that there was a wooden bridge over the Main here at a much earlier date.
In the 13th c. the bridge was given stone piers, resting on oak sleepers on the river-bed, but the roadway was still of timber. The bridge was exposed to constant threat from flooding and, in winter, ice, which led to catastrophes in 1235, 1276, 1306, and 1342 and regularly involved high maintenance costs.
The economic importance of the bridge – one of the great trade routes between north and south ran through Frankfurt – is reflected in the fact that after it was destroyed in 1235 Henry IV, son of the Emperor Frederick II, granted the citizens half the yield of the Royal Mint for its rebuilding and maintenance.
In addition the citizens of Frankfurt were given the right "in all time coming" to fell timber for the bridge in the Imperial Forest of Dreieich; and in 1300 15 Italian bishops assembled in Rome granted absolution to all who contributed to the rebuilding of the bridge piers after their destruction in a flood.
The bridge's two towers are first mentioned in the account of

the catastrophe of 1306, when the towers collapsed along with the rest of the bridge. They were subsequently rebuilt, and remained a characteristic feature of the bridge until they were finally demolished in 1765 (the Sachsenhausen Tower, copied in "Langer Franz", the tower of the Old Town Hall; see entry) and 1801 (the Frankfurt Tower). In the 14th c. the bridge was partly rebuilt with stone arches. By the 18th c., however, it was much dilapidated, and in 1741–44 a new bridge was built by Johann Friedrich von Uffenbach. Finally in 1912–26, following the canalisation of the Main, the bridge was again rebuilt. After being blown up in 1945 the bridge was given its present form in 1965. It now spans the Main with a total length of 237 m (778 ft) and a width of 19·5 m (64 ft).

At the north end of the bridge is a Crucifix with the "Brickegickel", a copy of a 14th c. warning sign. Tradition has it that from the 15th c. onwards those condemned to death by drowning were thrown into the river from this point.

There was formerly a mill on the bridge, at about the point where it crosses the island (the last remaining island in the river within the city). First mentioned in 1411, the mill continued in operation until the 1912 rebuilding of the bridge.

---

*Old Opera House (Alte Oper) J16 (B23/24)

The Old Opera House was ceremonially reopened as a concert hall and congress centre on 28 August 1981 – the 232nd anniversary of Goethe's birth – after much discussion about the rebuilding of this grandiose monument of the Gründerzeit (the period of rapid industrial expansion in the early 1870s) which was destroyed by bombing in March 1944. In 1870 a sum of 480,000 gold marks was contributed by well-to-do citizens towards the construction of an opera house on condition that the donors would be given priority in buying seats. An architectural competition in 1871 was won by Richard Lucae, later Director of the Academy of Building in Berlin, and construction started in the spring of 1873. After Lucae's death the project was continued by his assistants Albrecht Becker and E. Giesenberg, producing a building whose sumptous decoration concealed all the latest advances of 19th c. technology, and in October the Opera House was inaugurated in a splendid ceremony attended by the Emperor William I. The final cost of the buildings was ten times the amount originally contributed.

Location
Opernplatz

Trams
12, 17, 21, 22
(Opernplatz)

The exterior of the Opera House is in the style of the Italian High Renaissance. Apart from some panels of sgraffito decoration it is faced with Savonnières limestone, obtained from France in the form of reparations after the Franco-Prussian War.

Exterior

The Opera House consisted of the stage with its flies and machinery, the auditorium and the foyer. The foyer had a large central staircase which was omitted in the post-war rebuilding. The decorative painting of the interior was designed by Lucae and Friedrich von Thiersch, the representational painting by Edward von Steinle; the work was carried out by Frankfurt and Berlin artists.

Decoration

The sculpture was the work of Herold (figure of Mozart in the loggia), Schierholz (figure of Goethe), Kaupert (south

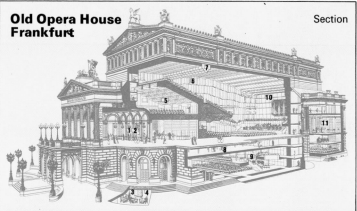

Old Opera House Frankfurt

Section

The Frankfurt Opera House, a neo-classical building built 1872–80 (architect Richard Lucae), was burned down after an air attack in 1944 and rebuilt as a concert hall and congress centre 1964–81.

1 Foyer (old-style and modern architecture).
2 Café, Im alten Foyer (seating for 140).
3 Bistro 1880 (seating for 150).
4 Jacques Offenbach French Restaurant (seating for 56).
5 Hindemith Hall (260 sq. m (2800 sq. ft), 340 seats).
6 Olymp (280 sq. m (3015 sq. ft), 500 seats).

7 Telescopic wall.
8 Exhibition areas (2775 sq. m (30,000 sq. ft) in foyer and corridors).
9 Mozart Hall (854 sq. m (9200 sq. ft), 700 seats).
10 Great Hall (including Olymp 2063 sq. m (22,200 sq. ft), 2500 seats).

11 Conference rooms (77–87 sq. m (830–940 sq. ft), 40–80 seats).
Telemann Room
Mendelssohn Room
Liszt Room
Schumann Room
Humperdinck Room
Pfitzner Room

pediment: personification of Comedy and Tragedy), Rumpf (north pediment: personification of Fate) and Hundrieser (chandelier with dancing youths).

The sculptural decoration of the exterior was restored during the rebuilding, with the exception of the figure of Pegasus, which was replaced by a new figure by G. Hüter, and the "Panther Quadriga" (by Frank Krüger, 1903) which topped the original building.

Most of the decoration of the interior, including the entrance hall and the former Painters' Hall (now the café, behind the loggia on the first floor), has been restored in its original form and colouring.

Auditoria

The central feature of the rebuilt Opera House is the Great Hall (Grosser Saal), which can seat an audience of 2500; it is multi-functional, serving equally well for concerts, congresses and dramatic or other performances on the stage. The adjoining Olympic Hall (Olymp), with some 500 seats, can be separated from the main house by a telescopic wall and used on its own. Other halls on different floors make it possible for several events to take place at the same time. The architecture (design and planning by Braun & Schlockermann and Partner/Professor H. Keilholz) is deliberately restrained, in contrast to the original style.

◄ The Old Opera House, now a concert hall and congress

The Old Opera House, restored to its former splendour

Old Town Hall (Altes Rathaus)   K16 (C25)

Location
Bethmannstrasse

U-Bahn
U 4 (Römer)

Trams
13, 14, 15, 16, 18
(Paulskirche)

The Old Town Hall was built between 1900 and 1908 (architects Franz von Hoven and Ludwig Neher) as an extension to the temporary office accommodation in the Römer (see entry). It stands in Bethmannstrasse, a new thoroughfare driven through the older part of Frankfurt.

The neo-Gothic Ratskeller was built adjoining the old house Zum goldenen Schwan (Golden Swan); to the west was the South Building, laid out round two courtyards; and next to the Paulskirche (see entry), linked with the South Building by a bridge supported by Atlas figures, was the North Building. The model for the new buildings, richly decorated and matched in scale to the old town, was provided by Renaissance urban architecture in Germany of about 1600. The interior decoration skilfully reproduces in every detail the style of the Renaissance. Reliefs and statues depict leading figures in public life and allegorical representations.

The two towers are copies of historic old Frankfurt buildings. The smaller of the two represents the Salmenstein Garden-House, the larger the Sachenhausen Tower of the Old Bridge (see entry), which was demolished in 1765; the latter is familiarly known as "Langer Franz" after Burgomaster Franz Adickes, whose office was for many years housed in the tower.

Ostpark (Eastern Park)   H/J19/20

Location
Ostparkstrasse/Ratsweg

The Eastern Park was launched between 1900 and 1908 by Karl Heicke. The pond in the centre of the park is probably a relic of the Riederbruch, a quarry at the foot of the Riederberg. In the south-west of the park is a garden containing species of plants under statutory protection.

Trams
18, 20 (Ostpark)
13 (Röderbergweg)

On the far side of the park, in Ratsweg, lies the Festplatz, a fairground which is the scene in spring and autumn of the traditional Dippemess, a fair and market at which the pottery of the Westerwald is sold.

Festplatz
(Fair-ground)

Beyond Ratsweg is the Ice Stadium (Eissporthalle), opened in 1982.

Ice Stadium

Ostzeile

See Römerberg

Palais Thurn und Taxis (Thurn und Taxis Palace)   J16 (B25)

The Princes of Thurn und Taxis, who acquired great wealth as Imperial Postmasters under the Holy Roman Empire, resided in Frankfurt only for a short time, but when they moved to Regensburg in 1748 they left behind them the most sumptuous Baroque palace in the town.

Location
Grosse Eschenheimer
Strasse

U-Bahn

U 1–3 (Eschenheimer Turm)

When Prince Anselm Franz von Thurn und Taxis was asked by the Emperor Charles VI in 1724 to transfer the headquarters of the postal administration from Brussels to Frankfurt he had the palace built by Guillaume Hauberat, to the design of Robert de Cotte, between 1727 and 1741, in spite of opposition from the town. After the family left Frankfurt the palace retained its post-office functions and was also used for the accommodation of great personages passing through the town. From 1806 to 1813 it was the residence of the Prince-Primate, Karl von Dalberg; from 1816 to 1848 and from 1851 to 1866 it was the meeting-place of the German Federal Assembly; and during the period of Prussian rule it was the headquarters of the Imperial Postal Administration under Heinrich von Stephan.
After the destruction of the palace during the Second World War only the entrance pavilions of the imposing Baroque structure with its three wings were restored. On the wall linking the two pavilions is a figure of Minerva (by Paul Egell) bearing the family coat of arms (a copy of the 1898 original) with the punning emblems of a tower (*Turm*, Thurn) and a badger (*Dachs*, Taxis).

The site of the palace is now occupied by the Fermeldehochhaus (Telecommunications House) of the Federal Post Office, one of the most important telecommunications centres in the world. It is the largest telecommunications exchange in Germany, handling some 1·8 million calls within Germany and 400,000 international calls every day. Here, too, are the switchboards for national and international exchanges of radio and television programmes. The exchange dealing with Telex, Gentex and Datex communications is in the Telecommunications Centre in the Zeil.

Telecommunications House
(Fernmeldehochhaus)

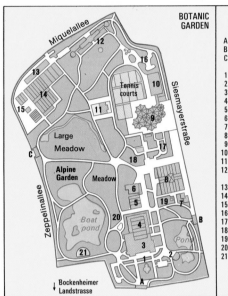

BOTANIC GARDEN

Palmengarten

A Main entrance, Palmengartenstrasse.
B Entrance, Siesmayerstrasse.
C Entrance, Zeppelinallee.

1 Flower border.
2 Music pavilion, open-air dance floor.
3 Assembly Hall (restaurant).
4 Palm-house, with viewing gallery.
5 Karl Egle House (subtropical).
6 Old work-shed.
7 Offices.
8 Plant-houses.
9 New plant-house (moist tropical).
10 Botanical collection.
11 Club-house.
12 Villa Leonhardsbrunn: gardening school;
   houses for Alpine plants, tower plant-houses.
13 Work-sheds, garages.
14 Ornamental plants.
15 Wintering house.
16 Large playground, miniature railway.
17 Irises and lilies.
18 Rose-garden.
19 Mediterranean garden.
20 Children's motorway, mini-golf.
21 Playground, park railway.

Map labels: Miquelallee, Siesmayerstrasse, Zeppelinallee, Tennis courts, Large Meadow, Alpine Garden, Meadow, Boat pond, Pond, Bockenheimer Landstrasse

Lush vegetation in the Palmengarten

* **Palmengarten** (Palm Garden)   H14/15

The Palmengarten was established in 1869 to house the famous plant collection of Duke Adolf of Nassau in Biebrich (Wiesbaden). The first assembly hall, with the large palm-house, in which a great variety of plants are now grown, was built in 1869–70 to the design of Fritz Kayser. The gardens were landscaped by Heinrich Siesmayer in 1872–74. Extensions in 1884, 1896–1908 and 1960, taking in the old Botanic Garden, brought the Palmengarten to its present size.

The plant-houses, with species from different tropical and subtropical vegetation zones all over the world, date from 1905–06. The Assembly Hall was reconstructed by Martin Elsaesser and Ernst May in 1929 and enlarged by the addition of a new west wing in 1953.

The gardens are of particular interest for their wide range of tropical and subtropical plants and for the many "theme gardens". They also offer recreational facilities (boat hire, children's playground, mini-golf, etc.).

On the north side of the Palmengarten, in Miquelallee, is the Villa Leonhardsbrunn, built about 1840 and renovated and altered in 1981, which now houses a vocational school for gardeners and florists.

Location
Palmengartenstrasse

Trams
17, 19, 21, 22
(Palmengarten)

Villa Leonhardsbrunn

* **Paulskirche** (St Paul's Church)   J16 (B/C25)

A friary was established on this site by Franciscans (Barefoot Friars) in 1271, and work began at the same time on the building of the church. In 1352 the friary was burned down but the church remained unscathed. During the 15th c., thanks to donations from the patrician families of Frankfurt, the church was renovated and enlarged. After the construction of the cloister in 1478 work began on an extensive rebuilding to the plans of Hans Lich and Arnold Hirt. In 1501 the construction of a new choir was begun. In 1510 the choir vaulting collapsed, though without injuring anyone; but Hirt, believing that some workmen had been killed, fled from Frankfurt. He returned soon afterwards, but in the meantime Hans von Bingen had been commissioned to complete the choir. In 1529 the Barefoot Friars, whose ideals were close to those of the Reformation, handed over the friary and the church to the municipal council of Frankfurt. The conventual buildings were used as a school and a library, and the church became the town's principal Protestant church.

By 1782 the church was in such a state of dilapidation that it had to be closed for worship. Demolition began in 1786, and in the following year Johann Georg Christian Hess began the construction of a new church to the design of Johann Andreas Liebhardt. It remained unfinished for many years, but was at last completed between 1829 and 1833 under the direction of Johann Friedrich Christian Hess. Since then it has been known as the Paulskirche. The first complaints about the church's poor acoustics began to be heard only a year after its completion.

On 18 May 1848 the German National Assembly took over the church. Its early meetings, however, had to be held in the

Location
Paulsplatz

Trams
13, 14, 15, 16, 18
(Rathaus/Paulskirche)

German National Assembly, 1848

Peace Bridge

The Paulskirche . . .   *. . . meeting-place of the National Assembly*

German Reformed Church while workmen sought to improve the acoustics by inserting a false ceiling under the echoing dome. In 1852 the church was returned to religious use. In 1867, after the fire which damaged the Cathedral, a fire-watching post was installed in the tower.

In March 1944 the church was destroyed. It was rebuilt in 1948 with a much-altered interior, and is now used for exhibitions and ceremonial occasions including the presentation of the Goethe Prize and the Peace Prize of the German book trade.

Peace Bridge (Friedensbrücke) L15 (D23)

Location
Baseler Strasse/
Stresemannallee

Buses
35, 46, 961, 972, 973
(Friedensbrücke)

Trams
11, 21
(Stresemannallee/
Gartenstrasse)

The Peace Bridge, the most westerly crossing of the Main in central Frankfurt, carries commuter traffic from the south-western dormitory areas of the city as well as traffic between the motorway and the Rhine-Main Airport (see entry) in the south and the Central Station (see entry), Trade Fair Grounds (see entry) and business district in the north. The bridge, in its present form of a plate girder bridge with five openings, was opened to traffic in 1951. The first bridge, built between 1844 and 1848, was a double-track railway bridge designed by the city's Chief Engineer, Eyssen. After the opening of the Central Station in 1889 the bridge, previously owned by the Main-Neckar Railway Company, became the property of the city.

At the south end of the bridge is a bronze statue of a docker by Constantin Meunier (1893).

Petersfriedhof (St Peter's Cemetery)   J17 (A25)

In 1452 a chapel dedicated to St Peter was made the parish church of the northern part of the new town which had developed since the 14th c. The chapel had been used since 1419 as a place of burial for the families who had founded it, and subsequently, following the closure of the Cathedral churchyard, a cemetery grew up round it. Among the Frankfurt patricians whose graves are in this cemetery are the Holzhausen, Glauburg, Hynsperg, Knoblauch, Limpurg, Melem and Cronstetten families. After the Reformation the cemetery was used mainly by Protestant citizens. On the south wall is the tomb of the engraver Matthäus Merian the Younger (d. 1687), on the west wall the tombstone of Goethe's father (d. 1782); the family grave of the Textor family, in which Goethe's mother is buried, was formerly in the cemetery but following a reduction in its size in 1911 is now in the yard of the Liebfrauenschule, surrounded by a semicircular colonnade.

After the building of the neo-Gothic church in Bleichstrasse (architects Dinklage and Griesebach) in 1892–95 the Late Gothic Peterskirche was demolished. The construction of Stephanstrasse cut off the south end of the cemetery; on the side facing the street is a copy of Hans Backoffen's Crucifixion group, the original of which is in the Historical Museum. (see entry).

Location
Between Bleichstrasse and Stephanstrasse

Tram
12 (Stephanstrasse)

Portico of Municipal Library
(Portikus der ehemaligen Stadtbibliothek)   K17 (C26)

The Municipal Library, built on the site of the old fortifications in 1820–25 to the design of Johann Friedrich Christian Hess (son of the Municipal Architect, Johann Georg Christian Hess), marked the eastern end of the residential district known as Im Fischerfeld. It had a neo-classical frontispiece borne on colossal Corinthian columns, to which were later added an inscription by Schopenhauer, "Litteris recuperata libertate civitas" ("The city, having recovered its freedom, dedicates this building to learning") and an allegorical relief by Friedrich Schierholz (1893–94). In the porch stood a marble statue of Goethe by the Italian sculptor Pompeo Marchesi (1840).

In 1891 an annexe housing book-stacks was built on to the library. Of the whole complex only the portico survived the Second World War.

Location
Schöne Aussicht/
Upper Main Bridge

Trams
11, 13, 16
(Rechneigrabenstrasse)

Postal Museum

See Federal Postal Museum

Prehistory and Early History, Museum of

See Holzhausenschlösschen

Preungesheim   D/E17/18

U-Bahn
U 5 (Preungesheim)

The district of Preungesheim, which originated in the 6th c. as a Frankish settlement, was incorporated in Frankfurt in 1910. The prison, built in 1886, became notorious as a place of execution during the Third Reich; the victims of Nazi tyranny are commemorated by an inscription by Ricarda Huch and a memorial by Karl Hartung.

Racecourse (Pferderennbahn), Niederrad   M/N14/15

Location
Rennbahnstrasse,
Niederrad

Trams
15 (Rennbahn)
21 (Triftstrasse)

The Niederrad racecourse was opened in 1865, with room for some 6000 spectators. A new stand was built on the north side in 1982, with covered accommodation for both seated and standing spectators. The Frankfurt Racing Club (Renn-Club Frankfurt), founded in 1863, organises some 25 race meetings a year (Grand Prix of Hesse, Frankfurt Grand Prix, Wäldches Race, Carl von Weinberg Cup, etc.). The charming little office in Schwarzwaldstrasse dates from 1865.

Rathaus (Town Hall)

See Old Town Hall, Römer and Technical Town Hall

Rebstock Park   J/K11/12

Location
August–Euler–Strasse

Trams
16 or 18 to Messegelände,
then bus 33

The Rebstock Park, south-west of the Bockenheim district, was laid out as a park only in 1958–62. Until about 1936 it had been an airfield, used by zeppelins as well as planes. The first landing by an aircraft here is commemorated by a memorial stone carved by Martin Elsaesser. An International Air Show was held here in 1909. The covered swimming-pool in the park was completed in 1982.

Rententurm   K17 (C25)

Location
Mainkai 30

U-Bahn
U 4 (Römer

Trams
13, 14, 15, 16, 18
(Rathaus/Paulskirche)

The Rententurm, which since 1717 has been hemmed in on both sides by the Bernus Wing of the Saalhof (see entry), was a defensive tower in Frankfurt's Late Gothic fortifications designed to protect the Fahrtor, the main entrance to the town from the Main. It is a square tower of four storeys, topped by a sharply pointed pyramidal roof with hexagonal turrets at the corners of the pyramid. Built in 1456 by Eberhard Friedberger, it acquired its present name in 1489 from the Rentenamt (the Municipal Treasurer's office) which was housed in the tower. The Fahrtor, also built by Eberhard Friedberger (1459), was demolished in 1840 when the road along the river-bank was constructed. The oriel window over the gate is preserved in the neo-Romanesque building on the north side of the tower.

*Rhine-Main Airport (Rhein-Main-Flughafen)   R/S7–10

The Rhine-Main Airport lies some 10 km (6 miles) south-west of Frankfurt city centre at the Frankfurter Kreuz, where two motorways intersect (Cologne–Munich and Hamburg–Basle). It is linked with the city by rail and by a new expressway. The largest airport in the Federal Republic, it is exceeded in passenger turnover, among European airports, only by London Heathrow. More than 70 airlines flying scheduled services and numerous charter companies carry a total of some 18 million passengers annually to or from the airport; and it is planned to increase the passenger capacity to an annual 30 million.

S-Bahn
S 14, 15
(Bahnhof Flughafen)

The Rhine-Main Airport was opened in 1972 after 15 years of planning (1950–65) and a seven-year constructional period (1965–72). The architects responsible for planning were A. Giefer and M. Mäckler. The total cost was some 1200 million DM.

History

For Frankfurt the Air Age began with the International Air Show of 1909, one of the high points of which was the landing of a zeppelin in the Rebstock area. The Rebstock site was used by the German Air Force during the First World War, and in 1926 became the Rebstock Airfield (Rebstock Park; see entry), which remained in operation until the opening of the present airport in 1936. In that year, too, the company running the airfield began a transatlantic service with the airships "Graf Zeppelin" and "Hindenburg", making 20 trips to South America and 10 to North America until the catastrophe to the "Hindenburg" at Lakehurst, New Jersey, in 1937 put an end to

The Rhine-Main Airport, an international traffic junction

the service. In 1939 the airfield was taken over by the Luftwaffe, and in 1944 it was destroyed by the U.S. Air Force. It was rebuilt as a military airfield in 1945, and civilian services were restarted in 1946.

The present airport is run by a limited company in which 45 per cent of the shares are held by the *Land* of Hessen, 29 per cent by the city of Frankfurt and 26 per cent by the Federal Government.

Passenger facilities

Beneath the airport terminal are a railway station and a garage with room for 6000 cars. Traffic within the terminal is separated vertically into Arrivals (ground floor) and Departures (first floor), and horizontally into sections A (Lufthansa), B (international airlines) and C (charter flights). There are 240 check-in desks, and passengers' luggage is automatically transported and sorted, under electronic control, by some 40 km (25 miles) of conveyor belts.

Shopping centre

Below the central area of the terminal is the shopping centre, with a supermarket, some 100 individual shops, three cinemas,

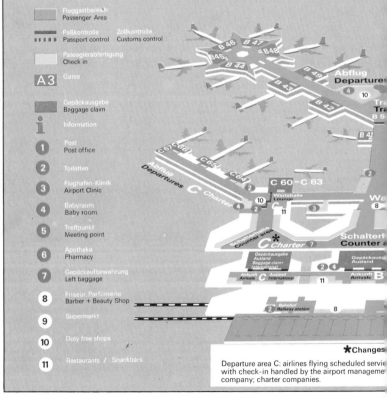

more than 20 restaurants, a discothèque, a chapel and a gallery for exhibitions, etc.

The airport's extensive spectator terraces allow waiting passengers and visitors to watch the busy activity of the airport. A number of veteran aircraft are on display at various points; a museum is planned.

Spectator terraces

In the Lufthansa freight-handling area to the west of the terminal is Wartungshalle V, a huge aircraft maintenance hall. Built for jumbo jets, this is the largest aircraft hangar in the world – 320 m (1050 ft) long, 100 m (330 ft) wide and 34 m (110 ft) high. The cost of construction was some 38 million DM. The roof is of pre-stressed lightweight concrete 8·5 cm (3·3 in) thick, with a span of twice 135 m (445 ft). Six jumbo jets (e.g. Boeing 747s) or 13 long-haul aircraft (e.g. Boeing 707s) can be serviced in the hangar at the same time.

Maintenance hall
(Wartungshalle)

The south part of the airport is occupied by the U.S. Air Force's Rhine-Main Air Base.

**Rhine-Main Airport
(Rhein-Main-Flughafen)
Wegweiser Terminal**

check-in arrangements:

Departure area B: international airlines flying scheduled services and handling their own check-in arrangements.

Departure area A: Lufthansa and airlines flying scheduled services with check-in handled by Lufthansa; charter companies.

97

** Römer

Location
Römerberg

U-Bahn
U 4 (Römer)

Trams
13, 14, 15, 16, 18
(Rathaus/Paulskirche)

The Römer, Frankfurt's historic old Town Hall, consists of a group of 11 burghers' houses on the west side of the Römerberg (see entry). The previous town hall, which stood on the site now occupied by the tower of the Cathedral and which was badly damaged by fire in 1349, was found inadequate for the elaborate ceremonial of the royal election which took place in Frankfurt from 1356, and accordingly in 1405 the municipal council acquired two adjoining houses known as the Römer and the Golden Swan. The former, whose name was probably derived from its occupation by Italian merchants attending the Frankfurt Fair, gave its name to the Römerberg (see entry), the square in which the fair was held. By 1878 the town had acquired nine more houses, giving the Town Hall its characteristic five-gabled façade.

At the left-hand end is a house first mentioned in the records in 1336 as Haus Laderam (probably from Lateran), another lodging used by Italian merchants which passed into the hands of the Alten-Limpurg family in 1495 and now bears their name. It was rebuilt in Renaissance style from 1595 onwards, and in 1627 received the addition of the fine external staircase in the Römerhöfchen, the starting-point of the election and coronation processions.

Adjoining the Limpurg house is the Römer, and beyond this Haus Löwenstein. Beyond this again are Haus Wanebach (first recorded 1373, purchased 1596), Haus Frauenstein (first recorded 1342, acquired 1843) and the Salzhaus (also acquired 1843). Of the houses to the west only Haus Silberberg survives unaltered. The Viole, Frauenrode and Schwarzenfels houses were pulled down to make way for the neo-Gothic and neo-Renaissance Old Town Hall (see entry).

The central feature of the Römer and the very symbol and emblem of Frankfurt is the three gables of the Alten-Limpurg, Römer and Löwenstein houses. Reconstruction of the houses began in 1405, and in 1414 the high vaulted hall of the Römer was ready for letting to the fair as a warehouse. The Imperial Hall (Kaisersaal) was completed in 1412; in 1741, when the Imperial Staircase (Kaisertreppe) was constructed, the hall was remodelled in Baroque style. In 1806 the Römer, with the Imperial Hall, lost its function in the ceremonies of the Empire. It was restored in 1827–28 and – on the initiative of the Städel Art Institute (see entry) and with financial help from citizens of Frankfurt and other art institutes – decorated with a series of portraits of German kings and emperors. Painted between 1838 and 1853 by leading contemporary artists including Philipp Veit, Alfred Rethel and Edward von Steinle, the 52 life-size oil-paintings span a thousand years of Imperial history from Charlemagne (768) to Francis II (1806). The coffered ceiling (1955) follows the pattern of the original ceiling of 1612.

The neo-Gothic façades of the Römer were designed by Mechel, the Limburg Cathedral Architect, winner of an architectural competition in 1889 – though the work, as executed, was a much-simplified version of his winning design. The details are modelled on old Frankfurt buildings such as the Nikolaikirche (see entry), St Leonard's Church (see entry), the Liebfrauenkirche (see entry) and the Leinwandhaus (Stone House; see entry).

An elaborately decorated lock on the Römer

Imperial Hall, the Römer

Römer Cathedral Area

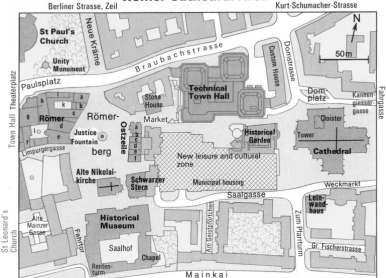

RÖMER – OLD HOUSES

a Salzhaus
b Haus Frauenstein
c Haus Löwenstein
d Römer (Imperial Hall on upper floor)
e Haus Limpurg
f Haus Silberberg
g Burghers' Hall wing
h Goldener Schwan
i Haus Wanebach
k Wanebachhöfchen
l Römerhöfchen
  (Hercules Fountain)

HOUSES IN OSTZEILE

a Grosser Engel (No. 28; to rear Kleiner Engel)
b Goldener Greif (No. 26)
c Wilder Mann (No. 24)
d Kleiner Dachsberg/Schlüssel (Nos. 22–20)
e Grosser Laubenberg (No. 18)
f Kleiner Laubenberg (No. 16)

The coats of arms on the brackets supporting the balconies reflect Frankfurt's relationships with neighbouring territories, cities of the Empire and Rhineland towns. Above are the coats of arms of the leading patrician families represented on the municipal council. Between the windows are figures of the Emperors Frederick I Barbarossa, Ludwig (Louis) the Bavarian, Charles IV and Maximilian, who all had particular connections with Frankfurt, and above them can be seen the heraldic eagles of the Empire and the city. To the right, on Haus Löwenstein, are the coats of arms of eight families of Frankfurt's town nobility; to the left, on Haus Limpurg, a personification of Frankfurt (Francofortia).

Beyond Haus Löwenstein, to the right, are Haus Frauenstein and the Salzhaus, which were destroyed in 1944 and rebuilt after the war in a style characteristic of the 1950s, with high triangular gables and mosaic decoration on the façade.

It is planned to reconstruct the Salzhaus as it was about 1600 as a magnificent example of Frankfurt timber architecture, with a ground floor of faceted red sandstone blocks and five upper storeys under a steeply pitched curved gable. The whole of the façade above the ground floor was faced with richly decorated carved oak panels which were preserved from wartime destruction.

*Römerberg   K17 (C25)

The Römerberg is an elongated five-sided square running from north to south between Braubachstrasse and the Fahrtor. Named after the Römer (see entry), the old house on the west side of the square which over the centuries since 1405 has been combined with other houses to form Frankfurt's Town Hall, it is bound up with the city's history and traditions more closely and intimately than any other square in Frankfurt. As early as the 9th c. fairs were being held and justice was being dispensed on the Samstagsberg (Saturday Hill), the eastern part of an open space which was originally within the royal stronghold. Kept free from buildings as an area for royal parades and ceremonies, it developed into the centre of Frankfurt's public life. In 1356 Charles IV's Golden Bull made it the place of election of the German Emperor, and in 1562, when Maximilian II was crowned, the Imperial coronation ceremonies took place in the nearby Cathedral (see entry). The Coronation of Francis II in 1792 was the tenth and last occasion on which the citizens of Frankfurt were able to watch the ceremonial accompanying the election and coronation being performed on the Römerberg, between the Römer and the Cathedral.

In the more recent past, between 1932 and 1939, the Römerberg was the scene of somewhat less spectacular events – the performances of classic German plays in the Römerberg Festival. It is now used for various cultural and political events, the annual Christmas fair and the Main Festival.

The square is bounded on the west by the five-gabled façade

U-Bahn
U 4 (Römer)

Trams
13, 14, 15, 16, 18
(Rathaus/Paulskirche)

Model of the Römerberg

Ostzeile

of the Town Hall, on the east by the Ostzeile (see below) and on the south by the Nikolaikirche (see entry). In the centre of the square is the Renaissance Justice Fountain (see entry).

In the years after the Second World War a number of architectural competitions were held and a variety of plans considered for the rebuilding of the area between the Römer and the Cathedral which had been destroyed by bombing in 1944. Some building was done in accordance with these plans, but in 1978 the city parliament resolved to abandon a redevelopment scheme based on a competition in 1962–63 and instead to rebuild the Ostzeile and the house known as the Schwarzer Stern (Black Star) on the east side of the Römerberg and hold yet another competition for the redevelopment of the remaining area between the Ostzeile and the Cathedral as a "leisure and cultural zone" combined with municipal housing. The official term for the area is Freizeit- und Kulturschirn – *schirn* being an old Frankfurt word for the open-fronted shops which were a common feature of the old town and provided popular meeting-places.

The new competition in 1979–80 was won by the Berlin architects Bangert, Jansen, Scholz & Schultes, who were then given the commission to carry out the scheme. In the housing development in Saalgasse the attempt is being made to combine the small scale of medieval dwelling-houses with the architectural forms of the 1980s; and in order to preserve the variety of the house fronts within the over-all unity of the street a number of leading architects who took part in the competition have been commissioned to design individual houses.

In accordance with the plan developed by the City Architect's department a beginning was made in 1981 with the rebuilding in traditional style of the Ostzeile, on the east side of the Römerberg, with a series of houses known as the Grosser and Kleiner Engel (Great and Little Angels), Goldener Greif (Gold Griffin), Wilder Mann (Wild Man), Kleiner Dachsberg/ Schlüssel, Grosser Laubenberg, Kleiner Laubenberg and the partly reconstructed Schwarzer Stern (Black Star). The topping-out of these houses, built in old techniques of freestone and half-timbered construction, was celebrated in August 1982.

With the rebuilding of the Ostzeile the Römerberg has recovered the dimensions it had acquired over many centuries. Although the individual houses are reproductions without historical authenticity they have, nevertheless, restored the historic pattern of the square.

Römerstadt   E13

U-Bahn
U 1 (Römerstadt)

Immediately west of the outlying district of Heddernheim, on the banks of the Nidda, is the Römerstadt housing estate, built in 1927–28 under the direction of Ernst May, which in quality of design and adaptation to the site set a pattern for later German housing developments. The name Römerstadt (Roman town) reflects the fact that the scheme is built on the site of the Roman settlement of Nida. It was part of May's plan for relieving the housing shortage after the First World War; and by the rationalisation of the whole operation (standard-type plans, fully equipped kitchens designed by Grete Schütte-

Lihotzky, the use of newly devised methods of prefabrication, a central-heating system) costs were kept down to a level which brought the houses within the reach of the lower paid. The gardens were laid out to the design of Leberecht Migges. The school at Im Burgfeld 1–13, built in 1928, was designed by Martin Elsaesser and Walter Schütte.

A number of other housing estates, some of them designed by architects of international reputation such as Mart Stam, were built on the outskirts of Frankfurt within the framework of Ernst May's development plan – all model examples of the humanisation of housing development and the functional architecture of the Neue Sachlichkeit (New Objectivity) movement. Notable among them are Zickzackhausen (Buchfeldstrasse, Niederrad: *zickzack* = "zigzag"), the Bornheimer Hang scheme (Ketteler-Allee, Bornheim (see entry)) and the Hellerhof estate (Frankenallee, Gallusviertel) (see entry)).

Rothschildpalais   K16 (C24)

After the demolition of Frankfurt's old fortifications the banks of the Main became one of the city's most favoured residential areas, and numerous villas were built there by wealthy Jewish merchants and bankers, who from 1811 onwards were officially permitted to live and to build houses outside the ghetto.

The mansion now known as the Rothschildpalais was built on the north bank of the Main in 1820–21 by Johann Friedrich Christian Hess, who sold it on completion to a merchant named Joseph Issac Speyer. It was bought from Speyer in 1848 by Meyer Carl von Rothschild, who had it enlarged in the following year by the City Architect, Friedrich Rumpf. At the end of the 19th c. it was used to house the Rothschild Library (founded 1887), together with the next-door house (Untermainkai 14), which was also built by Hess.

Periodic exhibitions organised by the Historical Museum (see entry) are held in the palace.

Location
Untermainkal 14

U-Bahn
U 1–4 (Theaterplatz)

Trams
13, 14, 15, 16, 17, 18, 21, 22
(Theaterplatz)

Rothschild Park   J16 (A23)

The Rothschild Park, in the angle between Reuterweg and the Bockenheimer Landstrasse, north-west of the Old Opera House (see entry), is now surrounded by high-rise blocks. It contains Georg Kolbe's "ring of statues" – seven bronze figures set between 14 pillars. Four of them (1939–41) are female ("Young Wife", "Herd Girl", "The Chosen One", "Amazon"); the other three (1945–48) are male ("Standing Youth", "Thinker", "Man walking downhill").

Location
Reuterweg/
Bockenheimer Landstrasse

Trams
12, 17, 21, 22
(Opernplatz)

*Saalhof   K17 (C25)

The name Franconouvurd first appears in the records in connection with an assembly held there by Charlemagne in 794. A palace (mentioned in a document of 822) was built by Louis the Pious to the east of the Church of St Salvator, probably on the site of a Merovingian royal stronghold; and

Location
Fahrtor

U-Bahn
U 4 (Römer)

Saalhof

Trams
13, 14, 15, 16, 18
(Rathaus/Paulskirche)

after the Treaty of Verdun in 843, under Ludwig (Louis) the German, Frankfurt became the chief royal residence (in effect capital) of the Eastern Frankish kingdom.

After a period of decline under the Salian line the development of the town was promoted by the Staufen kings (among them Frederick Barbarossa, who was elected king in Frankfurt in 1152). This increased importance was reflected in the construction of the new palace – probably a moated stronghold in the immediate vicinity of the Main – which is mentioned in the records for the first time in 1317 as *aula regia*, with the status of an Imperial fief.

In 1333, with the agreement of Ludwig the Bavarian, the Saalhof was sold to the Frankfurt patrician Jakob Knoblauch and was then converted into a lodging and warehouse for merchants dealing at the Frankfurt Fair. In 1696 it passed into the hands of two Dutch merchants named Bernus, for whom a

Bernus Wing

Cistercian monk, Bernhard Kirn, built the Bernus Wing (1715–17). This is a three-storey structure with a river front 60 m (200 ft) long, richly fenestrated with 13 closely set windows on each floor. In the roof are two high dormers with a pediment flanked by volutes and Corinthian pilasters, and there is a similar dormer on the west end of the building. At the angle of

Rententurm

the river front and the west end is the Rententurm (see entry).

Burnitz Wing

Adjoining the Bernus Wing on the east is the four-storey neo-Romanesque Burnitz Wing, built by Rudolf Burnitz in 1842–43.

Palas

Of the Staufen palace which had previously occupied the site it was possible to reconstruct two storeys of the Palas, together with the corner tower, the foundations of which, in rusticated stonework, are characteristic of military architecture about

The Saalhof, with the Cathedral tower to the rear

1200. Also preserved is the Chapel, a tower-like structure abutting the east end of the Burnitz Wing. Slightly trapezoid in plan, it has a rib-vaulted roof and a projecting apse.

Chapel

The Historical Museum (see entry) is now housed in the Saalhof and an adjoining modern extension.

Sachsenhausen

See Alt-Sachsenhausen

Sachsenhausen Bridge (Sachsenhäuser Brücke)

See Old Bridge

Sachsenhäuser Warte   M17

This Late Gothic tower, part of Frankfurt's outer defensive system, was built in replacement of an older wooden tower, demolished in 1425, designed to protect the road to Darmstadt. The tower was rebuilt in 1552. Within the inner ward are the remains of a Baroque forester's lodge built in 1767.

Location
Darmstädter Landstrasse 279

Buses
36, 960, 961, 963, 973
(Sachsenhäuser Warte)

St Bartholomew

See Cathedral

St Boniface's Church (St. Bonifatius)

The Roman Catholic Parish Church of St Boniface, built in clinker brick to the design of Martin Weber, is an example of the modern church architecture of the 1920s.

Location
Holbeinstrasse 70,
Sachsenhausen

Trams
17, 22
(Schwanthalerstrasse)

St Catherine's Church

See Katharinenkirche

*St Leonard's Church (St. Leonhard)   K16 (C25)

The Parish Church of St Leonard (R.C.), situated directly on the Main embankment, was founded in 1219 as a chapel dedicated to SS. Mary and George, built on a site presented to the town by the Emperor Frederick II. Of the original building there survives the richly decorated north doorway (1220), in the tympanum of which are figures of Christ with the Virgin and St

Location
Mainkai

U-Bahn
U 4 (Römer)

St Leonard's Church: stained glass . . .   *. . . and the main doorway*

John, St Peter and St. George. In 1317 a collegiate house was associated with the church. In 1323, after it had acquired the relics of St Leonard, it was re-dedicated to him.

The original Late Romanesque church was a flat-roofed basilica with four rows of arches in the nave, a square choir and two round east towers above the apses. Between 1425 and 1434, probably under the direction of the Cathedral Architect Madern Gerthener, a new Gothic choir was built, and about 1455 this was followed by the addition of a chapel (now the sacristy). Between 1500 and 1520 the nave was rebuilt by

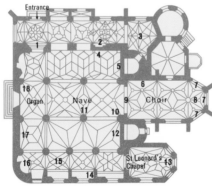

St Leonard's Church

1 Main doorway (Late Romanesque, 1220).
2 Romanesque side doorway (walled up).
3 St Salvator's Choir (Holzhausen Chapel, *c.* 1510; Baptism; "Madonna" by Steinle).
4 "Last Supper" (Holbein the Elder, 1501: copy).
5 Altar of the Virgin (Antwerp, early 16th c.).
6 Tree of Life fresco (16th c.).
7 Stained glass (mid/second half 15th c.).
8 High Altar (Bavarian, *c.* 1500).
9 Last Judgment (early 16th c.) in choir arch.
10 Madonna (*c.* 1420–30: copy).
11 Stone pulpit (16th c.).
12 Altar of the Cross (Lower Saxony, *c.* 1500).
13 St Leonard's Altar (J. K. Stieler, 1813).
14 Pietà (Early Baroque).
15 Double (Storch/Frosch) coat of arms (1520).
16 Madonna (Baroque).
17 Confessional (Baroque).
18 Flood levels.

Hans von Bingen in the form of a Gothic hall-church. In 1508 Hans Baltz took over the direction of building operations in the nave and built the little Choir of St Salvator (Salvatorchörlein). The church was completed only shortly before the Reformation, but by 1525 it was already beginning to fall into decay. With Frankfurt now Protestant, the religious houses steadily declined in importance. By 1792 the church was being used as a store. In 1808, however, a beginning was made with restoration.

Fragments of Gothic stained glass have been brought together in the five windows of the choir. The "Last Supper" by Hans Holbein the Elder (copy: original in Städel Art Institute; see entry) came from the Dominican church,. The Bavarian High Altar was carved about 1500; the Altar of the Virgin, from Flanders, dates from the early 16th c.

St Mary's Church (St. Maria)

See Deutschordenshaus

St Nicholas's Church

See Nikolaikirche

St Paul's Church

See Paulskirche

Sculpture, Museum of

See Liebieghaus

Seckbach   E/F19/20

The Frankfurt suburb of Seckbach is an old Frankish village which was incorporated in the city in 1910. The old part of the town, with half-timbered houses mainly of the Baroque period, is well preserved.

U-Bahn
U 4 to Seckbacher Landstrasse, then bus 38 or 43

The place first appears in the records in 882 as Sekkibah. Four hundred years later it was held by the Schelm family of Bergen, and at the end of the 15th c. it fell to the Counts of Hanau. The Town Hall (Hofhausstrasse 2) was built during their period of rule (though the masonry of the ground floor is later).

St Mary's Church (Protestant) was built in 1707–10, almost totally destroyed in 1943 and rebuilt in 1951. The Huth Park, on the north side of the Atzelberg housing estate, was laid out in 1911, in the time of Burgomaster Adickes; the Lohr Park (see entry) was established between the wars (1924–30).

In the south of the district, near the Riederwald housing estate, is the Pestalozzi School (designed by Martin Elsaesser, built 1926–27; Vatterstrasse 1–9).

Outside Seckbach, to the north-east, stands the College of the German Book Trade (Schule des Deutschen Buchhandels), a vocational training school for booksellers.

The celebrated collection of fossils . . .

. . . of the Senckenberg Museum

* * Senckenberg Museum of Natural History   J14
(Naturmuseum Senckenberg)

The Senckenberg Museum, famous for its collection of prehistoric animals, is one of Europe's most modern museums of natural history. In addition to the collections on public display it has research collections for scientific use.

When the Frankfurt doctor Johann Christian Senckenberg (1707–72) founded the Bürgerhospital in 1763 he also had in mind the idea of a "temple of science", but the idea was realised only after his death. Following a call by Goethe in 1815 the Senckenberg Society for the Study of Nature was established by a group of Frankfurt citizens in November 1817, and four years later a museum was installed in the Eschenheim Tower (see entry). The international reputation which this first museum won for itself was mainly due to the material presented by the African explorer Eduard Rüppell. With the move into a new museum built in 1904–07 to the design of Ludwig Neher, in a style modelled on the palaces of the Baroque period, the research collections were separated from the collections for public display.

The museum building in the Senckenberganlage is flanked by two wings in the same style, built by Franz von Hoven in 1907–08. The one on the right houses the Senckenberg Library, the one on the left the Physics Society (with observatory). The three buildings are linked by open arcades to form an imposing façade on the street front. Above the pediment is a figure, in beaten copper, of Cronos with his sandglass and sickle.

Since 1928 the Society has run an Institute of Marine Geology and Biology in Wilhelmshaven, known as "Senckenberg am Meer" ("Senckenberg by the Sea").

Ground floor: life in prehistoric times and the development of man, with fossils of wood maggots from the Black Jura; special exhibition of Egyptian animal symbolism and mummies of animals; large dinosaurs; a mastodon; extinct marine vertebrates (ichthyosaurs, finned lizards, sea crocodiles); rocks and minerals; the cave bear; dwarf elephants; large living mammals (whales, ungulates, predators); the ancestry of man; remains of early man.

First floor: Mammals I (simians, prosimians, predators); Mammals II (ungulates, marsupials).

Second floor: special exhibition, "Umwelt 2000" ("Environment 2000"); fishes of the Main.

Location
Senckenberganlage 25

Buses
32, 33
(Senckenbergmuseum)

Trams
18 (Messegelände); 17, 19, 21, 22 (Bockenheimer Warte)

Opening times
Daily 9 a.m.–5 p.m.

Southern Cemetery (Südfriedhof)   M17/18

The Southern Cemetery on the Darmstädter Landstrasse has been in use since 1868. The two pavilions flanking the main entrance, designed by Jacob Lieblein, date from that period. The chapel was built in 1888–91 under the direction of the City Architect, A. Koch.

On the north side of the cemetery is St Wendel's Church (R.C.), built by Johannes Kran in 1957. The walls, of rubble masonry 60 cm (2 ft) thick, borne on a few slender supports between an upper and a lower band of glazing, seem almost to hang in the air. The stained glass in the apse is by Georg Meistermann.

Location
Darmstädter Landstrasse
(near Sachsenhäuser Warte)

Buses 36, 960, 961, 963, 972, 973 (Südfriedhof)

St Wendel's Church

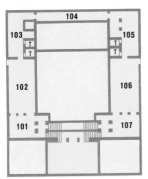

Senckenberg Museum of Natural History
(Museum of the Senckenberg Society for the Study of Nature)

SECOND FLOOR
Room 202 Molluscs (snails, shellfish, squids)
Room 203 Insects
Room 204 Spiders and crabs
Room 205 Animal communities (dioramas)
Room 206 Marine invertebrates
Room 207 Fishes
Room 208 Fishes
Room 209 Special exhibitions
F Festsaal (film shows)
R Ristorante Mario (two levels)

FIRST FLOOR
Recent higher vertebrates
(The arrangement in some rooms is temporary)
Room 101 Mammals I (simians, prosimians, predators)
Room 102 Mammals II (ungulates, marsupials, Edentata, scaly animals, monotremes)
Room 103 Animal flight; skeletons of large vertebrates (rhinoceros, zebra)
Room 104 Mammal embryos; heads of ungulates; reptiles and amphibians
Room 105 Birds III (nightjars, woodpeckers, passerines)
Room 106 Birds II (waterfowl, screamers, raptors, gallinaceans, cranes, gulls, terns, guillemots, auks, parrots, hummingbirds)
Room 107 Birds I (extinct species – moa, great auk, dodo; ostriches, penguins, storks)

GROUND FLOOR
1 Garden, with terrestrial sphere, giant ammonites and fossil tree-trunks – Entrance
2 Entrance Hall, with ticket desk and information desk; fossils from Black Jura, large mineral steps
3 North (right) Staircase Hall: fishes; fossilised animal tracks
4 South (left) Staircase Hall: Egyptian animal symbolism and mummies
5 First Court: skeletons of large dinosaurs (Diplodocus, Triceratops, Tyrannosaurus, Iguanodon, Stegosaurus, etc.)
6 North (right) Side Hall: extinct aquatic vertebrates
7 South (left) Side Hall: below, rocks and minerals; above, fossil invertebrates
8 Cross Hall: fossils of mammals (including specimens from Mainz Basin); special exhibition, Archaeopteryx
9 Rhynchnosaurid Cellar: skeleton of Trachodon; fossils from White Jura (Archaeopteryx)
10 Second Court: south wall – whales and dolphins; north wall – elephants
11 Outdoor display (planned)
12 Rear Hall: ancestry of man, research into human origins
13 Large West Hall: prehistory and early history of man
T Toilets

Senckenberg-1anlage Nr. 25

Städel Art Institute and Municipal Gallery   K16 (D24)
(Städelsches Kunstinstitut, Städtische Galerie)

The Städel Art Institute, founded in 1816, owes its origin to the Frankfurt banker Johann Friedrich Städel, who bequeathed to the city his collection of 474 pictures, which were first shown to the public in 1833, and a fortune of 1 million florins for the establishment of an art institute. The building which now houses the collection was erected in 1874–78 to the design of Oskar Sommer, who took as his model – as he did in the new Stock Exchange, which he designed in association with Heinrich Burnitz – the Louvre façades by Pierre Lescot and Charles Perrault. The extension on the south side was added between 1915 and 1920, and after the Second World War the side wings were rebuilt by Krahn (1959).

The Städel School (Städelschule) which has been associated with the Institute since 1829 is now known as the State College of Art. Among those who have taught in the school have been Passavant, Courbet, Steinle, Schwind, Hasslehorst, Beckmann and Baumeister.

In addition to its remarkable collection of European paintings of all periods the Städel Institute has a graphic collection of some 25,000 drawings and 65,000 prints, etc., and an art reference library. The Municipal Gallery (founded 1907) which is housed in the same building displays works of the 19th and 20th c.

Location
Schaumainkai 63

Buses
46, 961, 963, 972, 973
(Untermainbrücke)

Trams
11, 17, 21, 22 (Schweizer Strasse/Gartenstrasse)

Opening times
Tue.–Sun. 10 a.m.–5 p.m.,
Wed. 10 a.m.–8 p.m.

Staircase Hall, Städel Institute

Städel Art Institute

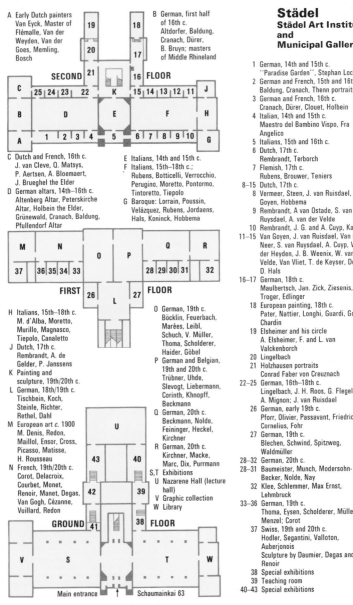

A Early Dutch painters
Van Eyck, Master of
Flémalle, Van der
Weyden, Van der
Goes, Memling,
Bosch

B German, first half
of 16th c.
Altdorfer, Baldung,
Cranach, Dürer,
B. Bruyn; masters
of Middle Rhineland

SECOND FLOOR

C Dutch and French, 16th c.
J. van Cleve, Q. Matsys,
P. Aertsen, A. Bloemaert,
J. Brueghel the Elder

D German altars, 14th–16th c.
Altenberg Altar, Peterskirche
Altar, Holbein the Elder,
Grünewald, Cranach, Baldung,
Pfullendorf Altar

E Italians, 14th and 15th c.

F Italians, 15th–18th c.;
Rubens, Botticelli, Verrocchio,
Perugino, Moretto, Pontormo,
Tintoretto, Tiepolo

G Baroque: Lorrain, Poussin,
Velázquez, Rubens, Jordaens,
Hals, Koninck, Hobbema

FIRST FLOOR

H Italians, 15th–18th c.
M. d'Alba, Moretto,
Murillo, Magnasco,
Tiepolo, Canaletto

J Dutch, 17th c.
Rembrandt, A. de
Gelder, P. Janssens

K Painting and
sculpture, 19th/20th c.

L German, 18th/19th c.
Tischbein, Koch,
Steinle, Richter,
Rethel, Dahl

M European art c. 1900
M. Denis, Redon,
Maillol, Ensor, Cross,
Picasso, Matisse,
H. Rousseau

N French, 19th/20th c.
Corot, Delacroix,
Courbet, Monet,
Renoir, Manet, Degas,
Van Gogh, Cézanne,
Vuillard, Redon

O German, 19th c.
Böcklin, Feuerbach,
Marées, Leibl,
Schuch, V. Müller,
Thoma, Scholderer,
Haider, Göbel

P German and Belgian,
19th and 20th c.
Trübner, Uhde,
Slevogt, Liebermann,
Corinth, Khnopff,
Beckmann

Q German, 20th c.
Beckmann, Nolde,
Feininger, Heckel,
Kirchner

R German, 20th c.
Kirchner, Macke,
Marc, Dix, Purrmann

S,T Exhibitions

U Nazarene Hall (lecture
hall)

V Graphic collection

W Library

GROUND FLOOR

Städel
Städel Art Institute
and
Municipal Gallery

1 German, 14th and 15th c.
"Paradise Garden", Stephan Lochner

2 German and French, 15th and 16th c.
Baldung, Cranach, Thenn portraits

3 German and French, 16th c.
Cranach, Dürer, Clouet, Holbein

4 Italian, 14th and 15th c.
Maestro del Bambino Vispo, Fra
Angelico

5 Italians, 15th and 16th c.

6 Dutch, 17th c.
Rembrandt, Terborch

7 Flemish, 17th c.
Rubens, Brouwer, Teniers

8–15 Dutch, 17th c.

8 Vermeer, Steen, J. van Ruisdael, Van
Goyen, Hobbema

9 Rembrandt, A van Ostade, S. van
Ruysdael, A. van der Velde

10 Rembrandt, J. G. and A. Cuyp, Kalf

11–15 Van Goyen, J. van Ruisdael, Van der
Neer, S. van Ruysdael, A. Cuyp, Van
der Heyden, J. B. Weenix, W. van der
Velde, Van Vliet, T. de Keyser, Dou,
D. Hals

16–17 German, 18th c.
Maulbertsch, Jan. Zick, Ziesenis,
Troger, Edlinger

18 European painting, 18th c.
Pater, Nattier, Longhi, Guardi, Goya,
Chardin

19 Elsheimer and his circle
A. Elsheimer, F. and L. van
Valckenborch

20 Lingelbach

21 Holzhausen portraits
Conrad Faber von Creuznach

22–25 German, 16th–18th c.
Lingelbach, J. H. Roos, G. Flegel,
A. Mignon; J. van Ruisdael

26 German, early 19th c.
Pforr, Olivier, Passavant, Friedrich,
Cornelius, Fohr

27 German, 19th c.
Blechen, Schwind, Spitzweg,
Waldmüller

28–32 German, 20th c.

28–31 Baumeister, Munch, Modersohn-
Becker, Nolde, Nay

32 Klee, Schlemmer, Max Ernst,
Lehmbruck

33–36 German, 19th c.
Thoma, Eysen, Scholderer, Müller,
Menzel; Corot

37 Swiss, 19th and 20th c.
Hodler, Segantini, Valloton,
Auberjonois
Sculpture by Daumier, Degas and
Renoir

38 Special exhibitions

39 Teaching room

40–43 Special exhibitions

Main entrance   Schaumainkai 63

German paintings of the 14th–16th c.:
Altdorfer, "Adoration of the Kings"; Dürer, "Katharina Für-
legerin"; Baldung Grien, "Two Witches"; Cranach the Elder,
"Venus"; Elsheimer, "Altar of the Cross"; Grünewald, "SS.
Cyriac and Lawrence"; Holbein the Younger, "Simon George
of Quotoule"; Master of the Upper Rhineland, c. 1420,
"Paradise Garden".
German painting of the 19th c.:
Böcklin, "Fanny Jananschek"; Leibl, "The Ill-Matched Pair";
Tischbein, "Goethe in the Campagna".
German Impressionists and Expressionists:
Beckmann, "Synagogue"; Kirchner, "Naked Woman with
Hat", "Barrel-Organist by Moonlight"; Liebermann, "Court-
yard of the Orphanage, Amsterdam";
Klee, "View of Cornfields"; Marc, "White Dog"; Nolde, "Christ
in Limbo".
Italian painting of the 14th–18th c.:
Bartolommeo da Venezia, "Lucrezia Borgia"; Botticelli, "Simo-
netta Vespucci"; Fra Angelico, "Madonna with Angels";
Moretto, "Madonna with the Fathers of the Church";
Pontormo, "Portrait of a Lady".
Dutch painting of the 15th–17th c.:
Jan van Eyck, the "Lucca Madonna"; Van der Goes, small
winged altar; Van Goyen, "Haarlemmermeer"; Matsys, "Male
Portrait"; Master of Flémalle, "Virgin and Child", "St Veron-
ica", "The Impenitent Thief"; Rembrandt, "Triumph of
Delilah"; Rubens, "Madonna with Saints"; Vermeer, "Geo-
grapher"; Roger van der Weyden, "Virgin and Saints" (the
Medici Madonna).
French and Spanish painting of the 17th and 18th c.:
Lorrain, "Noli me tangere"; Poussin, "Stormy Landscape with
Pyramus and Thisbe"; Watteau, "Embarkation for Cythera";
Goya, "Two Scenes from the Civil War".
French and Spanish painting of the 19th and 20th c.:
Degas, "Orchestra"; Manet, "Game of Croquet"; Monet,
"Breakfast"; Renoir, "After Breakfast"; Cézanne, "Landscape";
Delacroix, "Arab Horsemen".
Sculpture of the 20th c.:
Calder, "Red Lily"; Lehmbruck, "Seated Youth"; Picasso,
"Head of a Woman".

Stadtarchiv (Municipal Archives)

See Carmelite Friary

Stadtwald

N–R15–20

The Stadtwald (Town Forest), which has belonged to
Frankfurt since 1372, lies to the south of the town, extending
for some 15 km (9 miles) from Kelsterbach by way of Höchst
(see entry) to Offenbach. With its wealth of footpaths and
cycling and riding tracks it is a favourite haunt of the
Frankfurters. Within the forest, which has an area of 3952 ha
(9761 acres), are the Waldstadion (Forest Stadium; see entry),
a golf-course, the Louisa Play Park (at intersection of Mörfelder
Landstrasse and Niederräder Landstrasse) and the Goldstein

Tram
22 (Oberschweinstiege)

and Oberrad cemeteries. The amenity of the forest is, however, impaired to some extent by aircraft approaching and leaving the airport and by the motorways which run through it.

Wäldchestag

Between the Niederrad racecourse and the Waldstadion, near the Head Forester's house (Oberforsthaus), is an open space which on the Tuesday after Whitsun is the scene of a popular festival, the Wäldchestag. In its origins the Wäldchestag was probably associated with the driving of livestock into the fields after the winter or with the allocation of timber to the townspeople of Frankfurt.

Oberschweinstiege

The Oberschweinstiege, named after the sties for the pigs which were driven into the forest in large herds to feed on acorns, lies south of the Sachsenhäuser Warte on a peninsula in the Jakobiweiher, a man-made pond in the forest.

Staufen Walls (Staufermauer)   J/K17 (B/C25/26)

Location
Fahrgasse

U-Bahn
U 4 (Römer)

Trams
13, 14, 15, 16, 18
(Domstrasse)

The Staufen walls, which originally had a wall-walk on the inner side, were built round Frankfurt in the second half of the 12th c., with a dry moat providing additional protection. The walls followed the river-bank between the Old Bridge (see entry) and Seckbächer Gasse, with five gates on this side. On the north side of the old town their line can be traced from street names such as Holzgraben and Hirschgraben (*graben* = "moat"); there were three gates on this side. After the extension of the town and the construction of a new circuit of fortifications from 1333 onwards the Staufen walls served no purpose. Between 1583 and 1590 the walls on the north were pulled down and the moat filled in. The Wollgraben on the east side of the town, which had already been filled in, was assigned to the Jews as a ghetto; and when the Judengasse was almost completely burned down in 1711 the Jews were compelled to rebuild the section of the walls which had been destroyed. This section is still preserved.

Steinernes Haus

See Stone House

Stock Exchange (Börse)   J16 (B24)

Location
Börsenplatz

U-Bahn
U 1–3 (Hauptwache)

S-Bahn
S 1–6, S 14 (Hauptwache)

The Frankfurt Stock Exchange was built between 1874 and 1879 on a site which had originally been designed for the Opera House. The architects were Heinrich Burnitz and Oskar Sommer, winners of an architectural competition which attracted 39 entrants.
The façade overlooking Börsenplatz is 109 m (358 ft) long, with two projections flanking the central range with its portico of double Doric columns. The most interesting part of the building from the architectural point of view is the large trading

Trading in the Frankfurt Stock Exchange

hall (reconstructed 1955–57), which is some 32 m (105 ft) high, topped by a massive dome with an external height of 43 m (141 ft). The exterior, of limestone and tufa, is in the style of the Italian High Renaissance, with lavish sculptural decoration. On the pavilions of the central range are two groups of allegorical figures representing respectively War and Sorrow and Peace and Prosperity, with the coats of arms of Berlin and Vienna between them. On the middle block itself are statues symbolising the postal service, commerce, shipping, railways, industry and telegraphy.

The Frankfurt Stock Exchange is the busiest of the eight German exchanges, with an annual turnover of more than 40,000 million DM.

The present Stock Exchange can trace its origins back to the Burs, a body formed in 1558 by merchants trading at the Frankfurt Fair to fix uniform exchange rates for various currencies and thus obviate the confusion which had hitherto prevailed in the money market. The exchange operated at first on the Römerberg (see entry), and from 1789 in the courtyard of Haus Braunfels. The old Stock Exchange, designed by Stüler, was opened in 1843 but served only for 35 years before being replaced by the present building.

Tram
12 (Schillerstrasse)

Opening times
Mon.–Fri. 11.30 a.m.– 1.30 p.m.
(Free admission to visitors' gallery, with explanations)

History

** **Stone House** (Steinernes Haus)   K17 (C25)

The Stone House, on the north side of the Römerberg (see entry), a patrician house with a hipped roof, a wall-walk and

Location
Markt 42–44

Taunus Gardens

U-Bahn
U 4 (Römer)

Trams
13, 14, 15, 16, 18
(Rathaus/Paulskirche)

oriel windows, was built in 1464 for the Cologne silk-dealer Johann von Melem. After its destruction during the Second World War it was rebuilt in 1957–60 with an altered interior. It is now an art gallery run by the Frankfurt Art Union (founded 1829).
A stone figure of the Virgin which was destroyed during the war was replaced in 1972 by a copy. The coat of arms of the Melem family still hangs in the vaulting of the entrance gateway.

Leinwandhaus

There were a number of other Late Gothic mansions in Frankfurt, with a battlemented roof and corner turrets of a type similar to the Stone House. Among them was the Leinwand-haus (Linen Hall) at Weckmarkt 17, built before 1399, probably by the Cathedral Architect, Madern Gerthener. Originally designed to house the municipal weigh-house, it was used outside the period of the Frankfurt Fair for the sale of linen and hemp and was the great centre of the Hessian cloth trade. After serving a variety of purposes the building was used to house the archives of the Historical Museum (see entry). It was destroyed during the Second World War and rebuilt in 1982–83.

Taunus Gardens (Taunusanlage)

See Wallanlagen

Technical Town Hall (Technisches Rathaus)   J17 (C25)

Location
Braubachstrasse 15

U-Bahn
U 4 (Römer)

Trams
13, 14, 15, 16, 18
(Domstrasse)

The Technical Town Hall, planned between 1969 and 1972, was built by the firm of Bartsch, Thürwächter & Weber. The basis of the design was the plan for the redevelopment of the whole area between the Cathedral and the Römerberg which won an architectural competition in 1963 (among the other competitors being Ernst May and Walter Gropius). The architects were faced with the difficult task of carrying out their original conception in spite of a demand for accommodation fully two-thirds higher than originally specified and the need to incorporate in their scheme the Custom House built by Hebebrand in 1927 on the site of Friedrich Stoltze's birthplace, the old Haus zum Rebstock (House of the Vine) – thus reducing the area available for the new building. In the event the municipal council decided in 1978 not to proceed with the plan for the redevelopment of the Römerberg (see entry) but instead to rebuild the east side of the square in traditional style.

---

*Telecommunications Tower (Fernmeldeturm)   G14

Location
Wilhelm-Epstein-Strasse

Bus
34 (Fernmeldeturm)

The Telecommunications Tower, built for the Federal Post Office in 1976–78, is the tallest structure in Frankfurt (331 m (1086 ft)) and the highest tower in the Federal Republic.
The shaft and platform of the tower are constructed predominantly of concrete; the pinnacle which starts at 295 m (968 ft) is of plastic-coated steel. The "bulge" near the top, with six

The Stone House, an old patrician mansion ▶

Telecommunications Tower

Viewing platform
Open daily 9 a.m. to 10 p.m.
in summer

levels, is 26 m (85 ft) high and has a maximum diameter of 57·60 m (189 ft).
At 218 m (715 ft) is a revolving restaurant with seating for 220; above this is a viewing platform which can accommodate 300 people; and above this again is a cafeteria. On other levels are 120 directional aerials.
Telecommunications House: see Palais Thurn und Taxis

*Theatre   K16 (C24)

Location
Theaterplatz

U-Bahn
U 1–4 (Theaterplatz)

Trams
13, 14, 15, 16, 17, 18, 21, 22 (Theaterplatz)

Following the destruction of the old Theatre during the Second World War a new one was built between 1951 and 1963 – a handsome modern building walled with great areas of glass. This contains three houses: the Grosses Haus (1500 seats), the Kleines Haus (900 seats) and the Kammertheater (Chamber Theatre). A notable feature of the foyer is a large mural by Marc Chagall. In the glass-walled hall hang a variety of striking brass objects which can be seen from outside and give the building its characteristic aspect.

Three Kings Church

See Dreikönigskirche

Town Hall (Rathaus)

See Old Town Hall, Römer and Technical Town Hall

Façade of the new Theatre

Trade Fair Grounds (Messegelände)   J 13/14

By the end of the 19th c. it had become the practice to mount trade fairs and large exhibitions on a convenient site near the Central Station (International Exhibition of Electrical Engineering, 1891). After the development of the area around the station in the early years of the 20th c., however, it became necessary to find an alternative site.

Accordingly in 1907–09 a large exhibition hall was built near the goods station, based on a design by Friedrich von Thiersch which had won an architectural competition for the new hall, and a company established for the purpose began to lay out and develop the rest of the site. The hall – then the largest of its kind in Europe – has been used since the last war for a variety of sporting and cultural events (six-day races, concerts, etc.). Outside the hall, in the Ludwig Erhard Gardens, is the Mercury Fountain (see entry).

Served as they are by excellent communications, the Frankfurt Trade Fair Grounds rank among the most important exhibition grounds in the world.

The old Frankfurt Fair originated in the 11th c., developing out of the town's fruit market. The autumn fair was given Imperial sanction by Frederick II in 1240, and Ludwig the Bavarian authorised a spring fair in 1330. About 1800 Frankfurt lost its dominant position to Leipzig.

Among the leading trade fairs now staged in Frankfurt are the Book Fair, held in the autumn, the twice-yearly International Frankfurt Fair, the International Fur Show and the International Motor Show.

Location
Ludwig-Erhard-Anlage

Trams
16, 18 (Festhalle/
Messegelände)

Frankfurt Trade Fair Hemmerichsweg

Am Dammgarten

Rebstock car park

Hall 3

Hall 4

Hall 1

Re stau rant

Hall 2

CENTRAL

Hall 10

Emser Brücke

WEST

EAST

Hall 6

Hall 8

Philipp-Reis-Straße

Admin-
istration

Con-
gress
Hall

Hall 5

Varrentrappstr.

Galleria

Hall 9

Ludwig-
Erhard-
Anlage

Press
centre

Hall
7

Mercury
Fountain

Theodor-Heuss-Allee

City Central Station

Friedrich-
Ebert-
Anlage

N

Senckenberganlage   Hamburger Allee

Motorway (Westkreuz)

Frankfurt Fair

University (University)   H/J14

Location
Mertonstrasse 17

Trams
17, 19, 21, 22
(Bockenheimer Warte)

As early as the 18th c., thanks to the Senckenberg Foundation, Frankfurt had the makings of a faculty of medicine. Then in 1812, in the time of Prince-Primate von Dalberg, a University was established, but this lasted only a year. Further impetus came from various learned societies founded in the early years of the 19th c. (Polytechnic Society, Senckenberg Society for the Study of Nature, Academy of Social and Commercial Sciences, etc.), and eventually the University was established in 1914, in the time of Burgomaster Franz Adickes. In 1932 it took the name of Johann Wolfgang Goethe University.

The University buildings are in the Senckenberganlage, on the edge of the Westend district (see entry), in close proximity to the Senckenberg Museum, the Physics Society and the Jügelhaus. The Jügelhaus was built in 1906 (architect Ludwig Neher) to house the Academy of Social and Commercial Sciences; its façade is a copy of the middle section of the Electoral Palace in Mannheim.

The University – which since 1967 has belonged to the *Land* of Hessen – has 21 departments. The Institutes of Biology are in the Botanic Gardens, the Institute of Nuclear Physics on the edge of Rebstock Park (see entry), the University Clinic in Sachsenhausen (see entry); other institutes are accommodated in villas in Westend (see entry) because of lack of space in the Senckenberganlagen. The University also has a site in Niederursel (see entry).

Among notable teachers at the University have been the sociologists Theodor Adorno and Max Horkheimer, the neurologist Edinger and the chemist Paul Ehrlich.

Untermainbrücke

See Lower Main Bridge

Trade Fair Building

Upper Main Gardens

See Wallanlagen

Waldstadion (Forest Stadium)   O/P13/14

The Waldstadion, with its swimming-pool and open-air theatre, was constructed in 1922–25 (architect Gustav Schaumann, landscape-gardener Max Bromme) on land which had previously been a military shooting range. In 1960 two ice-rinks were placed in the area within the cycle-racing track. Soon after the opening of the stadium the first International Workers' Olympiad was held here in July 1925.

Near the children's swimming-pool is the Struwwelpeter Fountain (by Johann Joseph Belz), with themes from the well-known children's book by Heinrich Hoffmann.

Location
Mörfelder Landstrasse
360–362

Tram
15 (Stadion)

Bus
61 (Stadion/Kunsteisbahn)
Struwwelpeter Fountain

Wallanlagen (Rampart Gardens)   J/K16/17 (A–C23–27)

At the beginning of the 19th c. the bastions designed by Johann Wilhelm Dillich in 1627 and constructed in the course of the 17th c. to accommodate the old Gothic town walls to the military techniques of the Baroque period were levelled off and became a ring of municipal promenades known as the

Wallanlagen

Wallanlagen (Rampart Gardens). On the initiative of the Mayor of Frankfurt, Guiollett, and with the help of an annual contribution of 1800 florins from the Prince-Primate, Karl von Dalberg, the Municipal Gardener, Sebastian Rinz, and his successor Weber laid out a series of parks and gardens on which contemporary accounts bestowed high praise.

The last section was barely completed, in the spring of 1812, however, when it was destroyed by Napoleon's troops returning from their Russian campaign in the winter of 1812–13. Immediately after the Wars of Liberation the task of restoring the gardens to their former beauty began.

Heilig-Geist-Hospital

As a result of an Ordinance of 1807 protecting the area of the former fortifications the Wallanlagen have been almost completely preserved from encroachment by buildings. Only on the east side of the town, between the beginning of the belt of gardens, at the portico (see entry) of the former Municipal Library, and the still surviving remains of the town walls in the Upper Main Gardens, has the Heilig-Geist-Hospital (Hospital of the Holy Ghost) intruded itself. Built by Friedrich Rumpf between 1835 and 1839, it is a neo-classical building with three wings.

Upper Main Gardens (Obermainanlage)

On the south side of the Rechneigrabenweiher, a pond which cuts deeply into the Upper Main Gardens, providing a home for numerous waterfowl, is the Schopenhauer Monument, a bronze bust by Friedrich Schierholz which was set up here in 1895.

On the north side of the pond can be seen a marble bust of the 18th c. writer Gotthold Ephraim Lessing (by Kaupert, 1882).

Friedberg Gardens (Friedberger Anlage)

Between the Allerheiligentor (All Saints Gate), named after a Chapel of All Saints which was consecrated in 1366 and demolished in 1730, and the Friedberger Tor are the Friedberg Gardens, cut into two by the Zeil (see entry; clock-tower, the Uhrtürmchen). South of the Zeil, on the east side of the gardens, is a stone commemorating the synagogue destroyed by the Nazis in 1938.

North of the Zeil, towards the town, stands the late neo-classical house of Carl Fellner, the last Burgomaster of the free city of Frankfurt, who committed suicide when Prussian troops entered the city in 1866.

In the centre of the gardens is a memorial (by Petry) to Sebastian Rinz, the Municipal Gardener who created the Wallanlagen.

Odeon

At the Friedberg Gate, on slightly higher ground, is the Odeon, built by Johann Georg Kayser about 1815 as a museum in honour of Simon Moritz von Bethmann and now, after renovation by the city in 1982, occupied by a café. From the terrace there is an attractive view of the Bethmannweiher, a pond named after the great Frankfurt banker.

Close by is a bronze bust of Bethmann (by Eduard Schmidt von der Launitz, 1868) with allegorical reliefs on the base and the inscription "To the patriotic citizen Simon Moritz von Bethmann".

Bethmann Park

This park at the Friedberg Gate was acquired by the city in 1941 and opened to the public in 1952. Its flower-beds, green lawns and pond make it a great addition to the attractions of the Wallanlagen.

On the Friedberger Landstrasse stands the Hessian Monument, which until 1973 was at the Friedberg Gate. The monument (by Ruhl, 1794) was presented to the city by King Frederick William of Prussia after its liberation by Hessian and Prussian troops in 1792.

Hessian Memorial
(Hessendenkmal)

The Eschenheim Gardens, which extend from the Friedberg Gate to the Eschenheim Tower (see entry), are crossed at the Scheffeleck (end of Scheffelstrasse) by the line of the U -Bahn. From here the path, recently relaid, runs through the renovated part of the gardens.

Eschenheim Gardens
(Eschenheimer Anlage)

At the beginning of this section is a bronze bust (by Heinrich Petry, 1879) of Anton Kirchner (1779–1835), who wrote the first complete history of Frankfurt; on the base are allegorical reliefs.

In the cross streets on both sides of the Eschenheim Gardens, from here to the Eschenheim Tower, are numbers of handsome late neo-classical houses (Brönnerstrasse, Krögerstrasse, Blumenstrasse, etc.).

On the north side of the gardens is the striking Moorish House (Maurisches Haus), built in 1857 – evidence of the brief Romantic vogue in Frankfurt architecture in the mid 19th c.

To the east of the Eschenheim Tower is a monument erected in 1919 in honour of Philipp Reis (1834–74) and the demonstration of his telephone to the Physics Society in 1861.

The Bürgergarten, extending eastward from here, was re-planned in 1982, using architectural fragments from the Löwensteinsches Palais (now occupied by the Deutsche Bank). With its Medusa Fountain and its inviting seats under the shade of pergolas, this is the last resting-place before the

In the Wallanlagen: nothing is left of the fortifications but the name

Wallanlagen

Eschenheim Tower (see entry) and its bustling traffic.
At the foot of the tower, providing a kind of transition between the Eschenheim and Bockenheim Gardens, is a complex of fountains (by Hermann Goepfert, 1970), seeming isolated on this island in the middle of the busiest main road from Frankfurt to the north.

Bockenheim Gardens (Bockenheimer Anlage)

Farther west, extending to the Old Opera House (see entry), are the Bockenheim Gardens, restored to beauty since their re-landscaping in 1980–81. Half-way along is the Fishpond (Fischweiher).

At the near end of the gardens, on the north side, stands the Schwindhaus. a neo-classical villa built about 1845 for the painter Moritz von Schwind to his own design.

Between the public baths (Stadtbad Mitte) and the pond, standing by itself, is the Nebbien Garden-House (see entry), built about 1810 for the printer and publisher Johann Nebbien. Beside it is a 16th c. Italian well which came from the estate of Carl von Weinberg.

Opposite the pond, on the north side of the street, is the Mozartplatz, with a monument by G. Marcks (1963).

The Opernplatz, with the rebuilt Old Opera House (see entry), on the site of the old Bockenheim Gate, forms a link between the city centre and the Westend district (see entry). With the completion of the U-Bahn station in 1985 the square has become a pedestrian precinct and no longer interrupts the ring of gardens. The Marshall and Lucae Fountains add new accents to the square.

Taunus Gardens (Taunusanlage)

In this spacious expanse of gardens between the Opernplatz and the bank of the Main the figures of great Germans – Goethe, Schiller, Beethoven, Heine – seem oppressed by the tall offices of the great German banks: a symbolism which reflects the development of this free city of the Empire into present-day "Mainhattan".

Guiollett Monument

The Guiollett Monument commemorates the Mayor of Frankfurt during the period of French rule who initiated the demolition of the town's fortifications and the laying out of gardens instead. The monument, designed by Eduard Schmidt von der Launitz, was set up in 1837.

Beethoven Monument

The Beethoven Monument – designed by Georg Kolbe in 1926 but cast only in 1948 and unveiled in 1951 – stands on a bastion. The over-life-size bronze figure of a hero with the features of Beethoven is attended by two female figures, one calling to him and one meditating.

"Lachhannes"

At the point where the Mainzer Landstrasse meets the Taunus Gardens is a small fountain (by Johann Nepomuk Zwerger, 1859) depicting a grape-picker, popularly known as "Lachhannes" ("Laughing Jack").

Farther south is the Heine Monument, with a fine group by Georg Kolbe (1913) depicting two male figures, one striding out and one resting.

At the end of Grosse Gallusstrasse stands the Schiller Monument, a bronze figure by Dielmann (1864).

Beyond this, in the Gallus Gardens (Gallusanlage), is a memorial (by Benno Elkan, 1920) to the dead of the First World War, in the form of a mother bowed with grief.

Beethoven Monument   *Goethe Monument*

The Goethe Monument (by Ludwig von Schwanthaler, 1840) is an over-life-size bronze statue which stood from 1844 until the Second World War in Goetheplatz and was set up on its present site in 1952. The reliefs on the base depict allegorical figures representing Science, Drama and Lyric Poetry on the front and characters from Goethe's works on the other three sides.

Goethe Monument

At the end of the Wallanlagen, just before they reach the river and the Nizza Gardens (see entry), is the Fairy-tale Fountain, on the west side of the theatre. Designed by Friedrich Hausmann in 1901, it was not finally unveiled until 1910. Round the central figure of a girl on a high base are four tufa basins with upturned rims which originally bore bronze figures of children and fishes. Although these were removed during the Second World War the fountain is still one of the finest in Frankfurt. The model for the girl is said to have been a 19-year-old Frankfurt laundress.

Fairy-tale Fountain
(Märchenbrunnen)

Westend   H/J15/16 (A23)

In spite of wartime destruction, ill-conceived post-war rebuilding and a 1960s plan for redevelopment as a purely business quarter, with the property speculation and loss of housing accommodation which that involved, the Frankfurt district of Westend, between the city centre and Bockenheim, has contrived to preserve something of its original character, and it is still well worth a visitor's while to take a stroll round its streets.

Willemer House

History

From the middle of the 18th c. a garden suburb of small two-storey houses began to develop along the road to Bockenheim; then about the turn of the century prosperous citizens started to build large country villas in this area. With the demolition of the old fortifications between 1804 and 1811 ordinary middle-class houses appeared outside the ring of gardens (Wallanlagen; see entry) which had taken their place, and by the middle of the 19th c. Westend was a district of small detached or terraced houses. Then in the 1860s there was a more systematic development of the area, much of it speculative. After Frankfurt was incorporated in Prussia private builders created the pattern of streets and squares which still exists. The original main axis of Westend, the Bockenheimer Landstrasse, finally lost its character as a country road and became a city residential street. The large gardens were broken up and the land was more densely occupied by two- and three-storey villas, still owned by the same prosperous class as before. On the fringes of the district, particularly to the north of the Bockenheimer Landstrasse, blocks of flats, usually of four storeys, were built, giving the area a character which was largely preserved into the post-war period – though in more recent years this character has been somewhat altered by the intrusion of high-rise blocks (Zürich-Haus, BHF-Bank, Hochtief AG, Rhein-Main-Center, etc.).

Typical streets

Typical Westend streets are Niedenau with its neo-classical villas of about 1870 (among them the Villa Cronhardt, built by Christian Ludwig Schmidt in 1872), Guiollettstrasse, Feuerbachstrasse, Westendstrasse and Savignystrasse in the southern part of the district.
Of particular interest is the Livingstonsches Stallgebäude (Livingston Stables), an imposing neo-Renaissance building in Ulmenstrasse erected by Christian Ludwig Schmidt about 1880 as stables and coach-sheds and now occupied by a popular café.

Northern Westend

This is mainly an area of flats, mostly of good quality – for example in Oberlindau, Eppsteiner Strasse, Friedrichstrasse, Freiherr-vom-Stein-Strasse and Feldbergstrasse. Siesmayerstrasse, which runs parallel to the Palmengarten, is a street of prosperous villas, such as the neo-classical Villa Bonn, built in 1895–97 for the banker Wilhelm Bonn.

Synagogue

At the corner of Freiherr-vom-Stein-Strasse and Altkönigstrasse, in northern Westend, is the massive dome of the Westend Synagogue, built in 1911 to the design of Franz Roechle.

Willemer House (Willemer-Häuschen)   L18

Location
Hühnerweg 74

Trams
16, 17 (Mühlberg)

From the 18th c. onwards the Mühlberg was an area much favoured by citizens of Frankfurt for the building of summer-houses and garden-houses, since it afforded a fine view of the whole town.
About 1810 the banker Johann Jakob Willemer built a small garden-house in what is now Hühnerweg in Sachsenhausen; and from the upper floor of this slate-clad half-timbered house Goethe, then staying with the Willemers, watched the bonfires

In Frankfurt Zoo

lit to celebrate the anniversary of the Battle of Leipzig on 18 August 1814.
Goethe's friendship with Marianne Willemer inspired one section of his collection of poems, the "Western-Eastern Divan".

Women's Peace Church (Frauen-Friedens-Kirche)   G14

On the Bockenheimer Höhe in northern Bockenheim, looking on to the public gardens, is the Women's Peace Church, built in 1927–29 (architect Hans Herkommer) by Roman Catholic women's organisations as a memorial to the dead of the First World War.
Above the entrance is a mosaic figure of the Virgin as Queen of Peace by Emil Sutor. The Pietà in the crypt is by Ruth Schaumann, the stained glass by Pick (1962).

Location
Zeppelinallee 101

Trams
17, 19 (Frauen-Friedens-Kirche)

*Zeil   J16/17 (B25/26)

The street known as the Zeil runs from west to east through the heart of Frankfurt old town. Between the Hauptwache and the Konstablerwache it is a pedestrian precinct (extension eastward in progress). Numerous department stores and specialist shops make the Zeil one of the most important and busiest shopping streets in the Federal Republic.

S-Bahn
S 1–6, S 14 (Hauptwache or Konstablerwache)

U-Bahn
U 1–3 (Hauptwache)
U 4, U 5 (Konstablerwache)

127

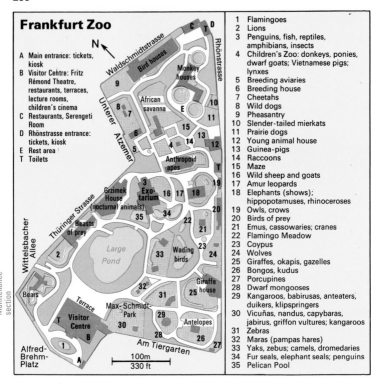

Frankfurt Zoo

N

A Main entrance: tickets, kiosk
B Visitor Centre: Fritz Rémond Theatre, restaurants, terraces, lecture rooms, children's cinema
C Restaurants, Serengeti Room
D Rhönstrasse entrance: tickets, kiosk
E Rest area
T Toilets

Waldschmidtstrasse
Unterer Atzemer
Rhönstrasse
Bird houses
Monkey houses
African savanna
Thüringer Strasse
Wittelsbacher Allee
Maintenance section
Grzimek House Exotarium (nocturnal animals)
Beasts of prey
Large Pond
Wading birds
Giraffe house
Terrace
Max-Schmidt-Park
Visitor Centre
Bears
Alfred-Brehm-Platz
Antelopes
Am Tiergarten
100m
330 ft

1 Flamingoes
2 Lions
3 Penguins, fish, reptiles, amphibians, insects
4 Children's Zoo: donkeys, ponies, dwarf goats; Vietnamese pigs; lynxes
5 Breeding aviaries
6 Breeding house
7 Cheetahs
8 Wild dogs
9 Pheasantry
10 Slender-tailed mierkats
11 Prairie dogs
12 Young animal house
13 Guinea-pigs
14 Raccoons
15 Maze
16 Wild sheep and goats
17 Amur leopards
18 Elephants (shows); hippopotamuses, rhinoceroses
19 Owls, crows
20 Birds of prey
21 Emus, cassowaries; cranes
22 Flamingo Meadow
23 Coypus
24 Wolves
25 Giraffes, okapis, gazelles
26 Bongos, kudus
27 Porcupines
28 Dwarf mongooses
29 Kangaroos, babirusas, anteaters, duikers, klipspringers
30 Vicuñas, nandus, capybaras, jabirus, griffon vultures; kangaroos
31 Zebras
32 Maras (pampas hares)
33 Yaks, zebus; camels, dromedaries
34 Fur seals, elephant seals; penguins
35 Pelican Pool

** Zoo (Zoologischer Garten, Zoo)   J18 (B27)

Location
Alfred-Brehm-Platz

Trams
13, 15 (Zoologischer Garten)

Opening times
16 Mar.–15 Sep., daily 8 a.m.–7 p.m; 16 Sep.–15 Oct. and 16 Feb.–15 Mar., daily 8 a.m.–6 p.m.; 16 Oct.–15 Feb., daily 8 a.m.–5 p.m.
Exotarium: daily 10 a.m.–10 p.m.
Nocturnal Animal House: daily from 9.30 a.m.

Exotarium

The Frankfurt Zoo, on the east side of the city, was founded in 1858 by Max Schmidt, a veterinary surgeon. Originally in the Westend district, it moved in 1874 to its present site on what was then known as the Pfingstweide. The large Visitor Centre, with its great hall, theatre, restaurant, conference rooms, etc., was built in 1876 (renovated 1957).

In 1915 the Zoo was acquired by the city of Frankfurt. With an extension to the east it covers an area of 11 ha (27 acres); wartime damage has been made good and it now has the most modern animal houses and open enclosures. The Zoo has an exceptionally wide range of species, including anthropoid apes, maned tamarins, maned wolves, okapis, leopards, panthers and many more. Since even the extended area of the Zoo proved insufficient, an outstation for hoofed and steppe animals has been established at Ginnheim in the Nidda Valley.

A feature of particular interest is the Exotarium which replaced an earlier aquarium in 1957, with a hall for different climatic areas, aquaria, a reptile and crocodile hall and an insect house.

The Grzimek House for small mammals also has a darkened room in which nocturnal monkeys, bats and other animals mainly active at night can be seen.

The Bird House on the east side of the Zoo, built in 1961 contains many rare species of the smaller birds.

To the north of the Zoo stands All Saints Church (Allerheiligenkirche), in Italian style, built in 1953 (architects Giefer and Mäckler).

Practical Information

Access

Frankfurt is a national and international traffic junction, with one of Europe's largest airports, Germany's largest railway terminal and links with the whole German and European motorway system. Access to the city, therefore, presents no problems.

Visitors arriving in Frankfurt will find it helpful to consult the following entries in this section: Airlines, Airport, Car hire, Car parking, Hotels, Information, Lost Property, Motoring assistance, Public transport, Rail travel, Railway stations, Taxis, Travel agencies, Youth hostels.

Airlines

Some 120 airlines have offices in Frankfurt. The following is a selection:

Air France	Kaiserstrasse 19–21, tel. 25 66-0/23 05 01
Alitalia	Rubensstrasse 2, tel. 60 94-0/6 90-40 85
British Airways	Friedensstrasse 1, tel. 25 01 21
Lufthansa	Am Hauptbahnhof 2, tel. 25 70-1/696-1
PanAm	Am Hauptbahnhof 12, tel. 23 05 91
Swissair	Am Hauptbahnhof 6, tel. 2 60 26

Airport

Frankfurt's airport, the Rhine-Main Airport, lies 9 km (6 miles) south-west of the city near the Offenbacher Kreuz where two motorways intersect. It is easily reached from the city centre by rail – a 10-minute journey, with trains every 10 minutes. The Airport is a busy junction, much used by transit traffic. Its present capacity is about 225,000 arrivals and departures a year; but after the completion of the new western runway this will be increased by some 20 per cent.

Airport information

To ring all airlines, freight services, banks, car hire firms, travel agencies, etc., at the Airport dial 6 90-30 51 or 6 90-1.

Rail services

S-Bahn line S 14 runs via Konstablerwache, Hauptwache, Taunusanlage (Taunus Gardens), Hauptbahnhof (Central Station), Niederrad and Sportfeld (Sports Field) to the Airport and continues via Rüsselsheim and Mainz to Wiesbaden. Line S 15 is a shuttle service between the Hauptbahnhof (Central Station) and the Airport.

At peak times there are trains every 10 minutes, at other times every 30 minutes. The S-Bahn station at the Airport lies 12 m (40 ft) underground immediately in front of the arrival and departure areas of the central part of the terminal.

There are several fast railcar services daily between Düsseldorf and Frankfurt Airport stations, calling at Düsseldorf Central Station, Cologne-Deutz, Cologne Central Station and Bonn. Some long-distance trains now run via Frankfurt Airport station.

Lufthansa Airport Express

Tel. 6 90-33 04.
Opposite the central section of the Airport terminal is an underground garage with room for some 6000 cars on three levels, and there is also a parking garage west of departure area A.

Parking

A well-stocked supermarket which also has film-developing, key-cutting, shoe repair and clothing alteration services is open daily from 8 a.m. to 9 p.m. (level 0, between arrival area A and the underground garage). There are also shops and boutiques of all kinds, including restaurants and snack bars, a drugstore, a chemist's, a clinic with its own operating theatre, a dental surgery, banks, car hire facilities and a chapel for all denominations.

Airport facilities

Open May–August 7.30 a.m. to 8.30 p.m., September 7.30 a.m. to 7 p.m., October–April 8 a.m. to 6 p.m.
Reduced admission charge for under-16s and disabled, no charge for passengers and children under six.
Flight announcements by loudspeaker (but difficult to hear because of aircraft noise). Conducted tours by arrangement.

Spectator terraces

A number of old aircraft are displayed on the spectator terraces and in check-in areas A and B.

Veteran aircraft

Antiques

There are some 150 antique shops and second-hand book-shops in Frankfurt, mainly concentrated in Braubachstrasse and Fahrgasse, the neighbourhood of the Cathedral and the Römer, and Alt-Sachsenhausen. Their wares cover a wide range, from junk which can be bought for a song to rare and valuable objects of museum quality.

Shops

An establishment that stands by itself is the Bunker in Sachsenhausen, which is stocked from cellar to attic with every kind of object which has been disposed of or thrown out, from sterling silver knife-rests or grandma's old soup tureen to a broken stone doorway.
Entrance in Schifferstrasse (corner of Gutzkowstrasse); open Monday–Friday 8 a.m. to 6 p.m., Saturday 8 a.m. to midday.

The Bunker

A flea market, at which everything conceivable except foodstuffs can be bought at modest prices, is held every Saturday from 8 a.m. to 4 p.m. (in winter to 3 p.m.) in the abattoir (Schlecht-und-Vichhof) at the corner of Gerbermühl-strasse and Wasserweg. Here professional dealers rub

Flea market

131

shoulders with amateurs, students, schoolchildren and some sharp entrepreneurs. If you don't mind the crowd and like rummaging about among junk, some of which is fairly squalid, you may conceivably make the find of your life.

Antiques Fair

An annual Antiques Fair is held in late summer in the hall of the Palmengarten (A to Z, Palmengarten; see entry), at which antiques and works of art are displayed for sale.

Banks

Opening times

In general banks and savings banks are open Monday–Wednesday from 8.30 a.m. to 1 p.m. and 2 p.m. to 4 p.m., Thursday to 4.30 p.m. and Friday to 3.30 p.m.

Changing money

Money can be changed in all banks and savings banks with public counters, in the head post offices in the city centre and at the Airport, and also in the large department stores and hotels (though in this last case sometimes at a less favourable rate).

Late opening

Deutsche Verkehrs-Kredit-Bank:
Hauptbahnhof (Central Station), south side, daily 6.30 a.m. to 10 p.m.
Central Station, shopping arcade, daily 8 a.m. to 8 p.m.
Airport, arrival area B 8, daily 7.30 a.m. to 9.30 p.m.

Commerzbank:
Airport, arrival area B 6, daily 7.30 a.m. to 9.15 p.m.

Boat hire

In summer canoes, pedalos and rowing-boats can be hired at the Iron Bridge on the Deutschherrnufer and on the pond in the Palmengarten (A to Z, Palmengarten; see entry).

Harry's Boothaus,
Deutschherrnufer, Upper Main Bridge
Boats can be hired from 10 a.m. to dusk.
Trams: 11, 16 (Frankensteiner Platz)

Bootsverleih Motzheim,
Iron Bridge (Sachsenhausen side)
Boats hired from 11 a.m. according to weather; in summer to 8 p.m.
Buses: 46, 961, 963, 972, 973 (Eiserner Steg)

Boutiques

While the large department stores are almost all to be found in the Zeil (at present in course of development as a pedestrian precinct) and in general set out to meet the demand for textiles and other consumer goods at reasonable prices, the more exclusive and more expensive boutiques still dominate, as in the past, the area around the Opernplatz, Goethestrasse,

Grosse Bockenheimer Strasse (the "Fressgass" or "Guzzling Street"), Schillerstrasse, Steinweg, Goetheplatz, Rathenauplatz and Kaiserstrasse. Here are to be found the shops of the great French and Italian fashion houses and the expensive perfumeries which sell the products of internationally renowned cosmetic firms. In the streets running down from the Zeil to the Römerberg (pedestrian precinct), however, there are boutiques in all price ranges selling fashion articles for both men and women, gifts, books, leather goods, items of furniture, etc.

Outside the city centre, the Leipziger Strasse in Bockenheim, the Berger Strasse in Bornheim and the Schweizer Strasse in Sachsenhausen have developed into attractive shopping streets.

Camping

Campingplatz/Bootshaus Maul,
Niederräder Ufer 2 (on the left bank of the Main, near the railway bridge), tel. 67 38 46

Camping sites

Campingplatz Heddernheim,
An der Sandelmühle 35 (on the right bank of the Nidda), tel. 57 03 32

Car hire

Avis
Niddastrasse 46–48, tel. 23 01 01
Hanauer Landstrasse 66, tel. 49 00 36
Frankenallee 41, tel. 73 03 91
Airport, tel. 6 90 27 77

Avis

Europcar
Wiesenhüttenplatz 36, tel. 23 40 02-5
Airport, tel. 6 90 51 07

Europcar

Hertz
Hanauer Landstrasse 106, tel. 43 92 48
Mainzer Landstrasse 139, tel. 23 31 51
Airport, tel. 6 90 50 11

Hertz

InterRent
Stephanstrasse 15, tel. 29 10 28
Schloss-strasse 34–36, tel. 77 50 33
Hanauer Landstrasse 334, tel. 42 30 25
Borsigallee 31, tel. 41 10 08

InterRent

Car parking

Airport, Arrival areas A, B and C
Open: 24 hours a day

Multi-storey car parks

133

Practical Information

Central Station
Poststrasse
Approach by Düsseldorfer Strasse, Taunusstrasse, Münchener Strasse and Baseler Strasse
Open: 24 hours a day

Old Opera House
Opernplatz 1 a
Approach by Taunusanlage, Bockenheimer Anlage
Open: 24 hours a day

Hauptwache
Kornmarkt 10
Approach by Berliner Strasse
Open: 24 hours a day

Kaiserplatz
Bethmannstrasse 50–54
Approach by Friedensstrasse
Open: 24 hours a day

Am Theater
Wilhelm-Leuschner-Strasse 1
Approach by Gallusanlage, Untermainanlage
Open: 24 hours a day

Junghofstrasse
Junghofstrasse 16
Approach from Goetheplatz and Taunusanlage or Neue Mainzer Strasse
Open: Mon.–Sat. 6.30 a.m. to midnight
Closed: Sundays and public holidays

Stock Exchange
Meisengasse
Approach by Hochstrasse, Zwingergasse
Open: Mon.–Sat. 6.30 a.m. to 1 a.m., Sun. and public holidays 10 a.m. to 1 a.m.

Stadtbad Mitte (Public Baths)
Taubenstrasse 7
Approach by Eschenheim Tower
Open: 24 hours a day

Kaufhaus Hertie
Brönnerstrasse
Approach by Eschenheim Tower, Bleichstrasse
Open: Mon.–Fri. 7 a.m. to 7 p.m., Sat. 7 a.m. to 2.30 p.m. (or 6.30 p.m. on the first Saturday of every month)

Am Gericht
Klapperfeldstrasse 8
Approach by Bleichstrasse and Seilerstrasse
Open: Mon.–Sat. 6.30 a.m. to 8 p.m.
Closed: Sundays and public holidays

Konstablerwache
Reineckstrasse 7
Approach by Berliner Strasse, Hasengasse
Open: Mon.–Sat. 6.30 a.m. to 10 p.m.
Closed: Sundays and public holidays

Am Gewerkschaftshaus
Gutleutstrasse 87
Approach by Gallusanlage
Open: Mon.–Sat. 6.30 a.m. to 10 p.m.
Closed: Sundays and public holidays

Platz der Republik
Westendstrasse 1
Approach by Mainzer Landstrasse
Open: 24 hours a day

Moselstrasse 41–43
Approach by Karlstrasse, Niddastrasse (from Central Station)
Open: Mon.–Fri. 6.30 a.m. to 10 p.m., Sat. 730 a.m. to 7 p.m.
Closed: Sundays and public holidays

Gutleut
Gutleutstrasse 49
Approach by Gallusanlage
Open: 24 hours a day

City-Parkhaus
Querstrasse
Approach by Oeder Weg
Open: Mon.–Sat. 6 a.m. to 9 p.m.
Closed: Sundays and public holidays

Parkebene Römer
Domstrasse
Approach by Braubachstrasse
At present closed because of construction work on Römerberg

Senckenberganlage
Hamburger Alle 2–10
Approach by Friedrich-Ebert-Anlage
Open: 24 hours a day

BfG-Tiefgarage
Theaterplatz 2
Approach by Neue Mainzer Landstrasse
Open: daily 6 a.m. to midnight

Alt-Sachsenhausen
Heisterstrasse 1–3
Approach by Darmstädter Landstrasse
Open: 24 hours a day

Nordwest-Zentrum
Erich-Ollenhauer-Ring
Approach by Rosa-Luxembourg-Strasse (urban motorway)
Open: 24 hours a day

Chemists

There are numerous chemists' shops in every part of Frankfurt, so that there is no difficulty in obtaining any medicines required. For a list of chemists, consult the local telephone directory or the "yellow pages" (die gelben Seiten) directory.

There are rota arrangements for keeping certain chemists' shops open at night and on Sundays and public holidays. To find out which chemists are on duty dial 1150 (tape-recorded information). All chemists display after closing time a notice giving the name of the nearest chemist who is open.

Cider bars (Apfelweinwirtschaften)

"Ebbelwei"

The cider (*Ebbelwei* or *Apfelwein*, "apple wine") of which the people of Frankfurt are so fond, has been drunk there since the middle of the 18th c., and the typical Frankfurt cider bars have an equally long history. A garland of fir branches hung outside a bar indicates that it brews its own cider. The cider is served in a grey pottery jug called a *Bembel* and drunk in a ribbed or lozenge-patterned glass tankard (which is, incidentally, a popular souvenir of Frankfurt). In summer the habitués like to drink out of doors at long tables under shady trees, sitting companionably close together with their friends – or with anyone else with whom they can start a conversation in this friendly and democratic atmosphere.

A distinction is made between different types of cider. It is described as "sweet" (*Süsser*) when it is freshly made in autumn and not yet fermented; and this then develops into *Rauscher*, later into *Heller* and finally into *Alter*. The addition of crab-apples to the brew produces *Speierling*.

Cider bars are found not only in Sachsenhausen but also in the city centre and in many of the outer districts. Some of the bars have curious dialect names which even a visitor from some other part of Germany, and even more so a foreign visitor, may have difficulty in interpreting.

A selection of some of the best-known cider bars:

Apfelwein-Klaus,
Meisengasse (near Opernplatz)
Trams: 12, 17, 21, 22 (Opernplatz)

Zum Gemalten Haus,
Schweizer Strasse 67, Sachsenhausen
Trams: 17, 22 (Schwanthalerstrasse)

Adolf Wagner,
Schweizer Strasse 71, Sachsenhausen
Trams: 17, 22 (Schwanthalerstrasse)

Buchscheer,
Gablonzer Strasse (corner of Stresemannalle), Sachsenhausen
Tram: 22 (Louisa). Bus: 35 (Louisa)

Zur Schönen Müllerin,
Baumweg 12, Nordend
U-Bahn: U 4 (Merianplatz)

Solzer Karl,
Berger Strasse 260, Alt-Bornheim
U-Bahn: U 4 (Seckbacher Landstrasse terminus)

In a Frankfurt cider bar

Zur Eulenburg,
Eulengasse 46, Alt-Bornheim
U-Bahn: U 4 (Seckbacher Landstrasse terminus)

Zum Rad,
Leonhardsgasse 2/Wilhelmshöher Strasse, Seckenbach
Bus: 43 (Draisbornstrasse)

Friedberger Warte,
Friedberger Landstrasse 360
Buses: 34, 38, 69 (Friedberger Warte)

Momberger,
Alt-Heddernheim 13
U-Bahn: U 1–3 (Heddernheim)

Germania,
Textorstrasse 18
Trams: 11, 17 (Textorstrasse)

In Alt-Sachsenhausen

Fichtekränzi,
Wallstrasse 5
Buses: 36, 960 (Elisabethenstrasse)

Atschel,
Wallstrasse 7
Buses: 36, 960 (Elisabethenstrasse)

Aprikösie,
Neuer Wall
Trams: 11, 16 (Frankensteiner Platz)

Klaane Sachsehäuser,
Neuer Wall 11
Trams: 11, 16 (Frankensteiner Platz)

Hinnerkopp,
Grosse Rittergasse 57
Trams: 11, 16 (Frankensteiner Platz)

Zum Grauen Bock,
Grosse Rittergasse 30
Trams: 11, 16 (Frankensteiner Platz)

Altänchen,
Grosse Rittergasse 112
Buses: 36, 960 (Elisabethenstrasse)

Kuhhirtenturm,
Grosse Rittergasse 114
Buses: 36, 960 (Elisabethenstrasse)

Cinemas

Frankfurt has 78 first-run and repertory cinemas, most of them in the neighbourhood of the Hauptwache and in Kaiserstrasse. To find out what's on, consult the programme listings given weekly in the Press (e.g. in the "Frankfurter Allgemeine Zeitung" on Fridays) or ring 1 15 13 or 1 15 14.

Communal Cinema
(Kommunales Kino)

A special Frankfurt institution is the Communal Cinema in the Historical Museum (see entry) in Saalgasse (on the Römerberg), which shows several different programmes daily of films which in some way are notable or interesting. Performances begin at 5.30 p.m., 8 p.m. and 10 p.m., with some special performances at 3 p.m.

Consulates

United Kingdom

Consulate-General
Bockenheimer Landstrasse 51,
tel. 72 04 06

United States

Consulate-General
Siesmayerstrasse 21,
tel. 74 00 71

Cuisine

Specialities

Frankfurt is no less celebrated for its sausages (Frankfurters), which earned the highest distinctions at the Chicago World's Fair in 1893, and its cider (Cider bars; see entry) than for its

Römer or Paulskirche or Cathedral. And the essential accompaniment to the cider, *Handkäs mit Musik* (the "music" which goes with the cheese being a composition of oil and vinegar, pepper and salt and finely chopped onions), has achieved a reputation extending well beyond the boundaries of Hessen.

It must be admitted, however, that apart from these three items there are few distinctively Frankfurt dishes. One typical feature of the menu is green sauce (*Grie Soss*, in standard German *Grüne Sosse*), which consists of at least seven finely chopped herbs (chives, parsley, chervil, cress, sorrel, borage and pimpernel), chopped boiled eggs, salt, wine vinegar or lemon and plenty of oil, and goes very well with boiled meat or fish, poached eggs or potatoes in their jackets; it is said that Goethe thought very highly of this sauce. Another favourite Frankfurt dish is *Rippchen mit Kraut* (pork rib with Sauerkraut). And by way of sweet there is the *Frankfurter Kranz*, a cake containing three layers of butter cream, sprinkled with crumbs of cracknel and decorated with cherries and pistachios.

Typical dishes

Apart from its local dishes Frankfurt can offer a varied cuisine – German, foreign and sometimes highly exotic – with a high standard of cooking and a touch of international flair. See below, Restaurants.

Cultural institutions

Amerika-Haus,
Staufenstrasse 1
Trams: 12, 17, 21, 22 (Opernplatz)

German-Italian Society (Deutsch-Italienische Vereinigung),
Arndtstrasse 12
Tram: 19 (Kettenhofweg)

German-French Society (Deutsch-Französische Gesellschaft),
Bockenheimer Landstrasse 22
Trams: 12, 17, 21, 22 (Opernplatz)

German-Australian Society (Deutsch-Australische Gesellschaft),
Reuterweg 14
Trams: 12, 17, 21, 22 (Opernplatz)

German-Ibero-American Society (Deutsch-Ibero-Amerikanische Gesellschaft),
Gräfstrasse 83
Trams: 17, 19, 21, 22 (Bockenheimer Warte)

Institut Français (Französisches Institut),
Am Leonhardsbrunnen 4
Buses: 32, 33 (Ditmarstrasse)

Emergency calls

Tel. 79 20-200

Medical emergency service

Practical Information

First aid	1 12
Fire service	1 12
Police	1 10

Events

January	International Domestic Textiles Fair (trade only)
February	Shrove Tuesday celebrations (Fairs; see entry) Music Fair (international fair for musical instruments, electronic music, etc.: trade only) International Consumer Goods Fair (trade only)
March	4 × bau frankfurt (Building Show, alternate years)
April	Dippemess (Fairs; see entry) International Fur Show (trade only)
May	Wäldchestag (Tuesday after Whitsun: Fairs; see entry) International Clothing Textiles Fair (trade only) "Round the Henninger Tower" (international cycle race)
June	"Frankfurt Summertime" – song recitals, concerts and drama in squares and parks (Wed., Sat. and Sun.) Rose and Light Festival in Palmengarten Chemical Industries Fair (every three years: trade only)
July	Höchst Castle Festival (Fairs; see entry) Main Festival (Fairs; see entry) "Frankfurt Summertime" (see June)
August	Summer Flower Festival in Palmengarten Bernemer Kerb (Fairs; see entry) Sachsenhausen Fountain Festival International Consumer Goods Fair (trade only) "Frankfurt Summertime" (see June)
September	Open Day (Römerberg, Karlsplatz) Bergen Market (Fairs; see entry) Dippemess (Fairs; see entry) International Motor Show (alternate years) Frankfurt Festival in Old Opera House (varied programme, mainly musical) Frankfurt Grand Prix (flat race, Niederrad racecourse)
October	Six-Day Race in Festhalle, Trade Fair Grounds International Book Fair Hotel and Restaurant Fair (alternate years: trade only)
November	International Clothing Textiles Fair Home and Leisure Show and Tourism Show (two related trade fairs held at the same time)
December	Christmas Market (Fairs; see entry)
	For information about events throughout the year, see What's on (below).

Excursions

There is much to see not only in Frankfurt itself but also in the beautiful and romantic surroundings. The Taunus hills, the Spessart and the Odenwald are practically on the city's doorstep, easily accessible by public transport (see Public transport, FVV). Some visitors may be attracted by a walk on some of the many waymarked footpaths in the surrounding countryside – for example on the Feldberg, Frankfurt's domestic mountain; others may prefer a drive to some of the places of interest within easy range, or perhaps a boat trip on the Main and the Rhine. If you like an organised trip rather than going on your own, there is a wide choice of excursions run by the German Federal Railways, bus companies and travel agencies. There are also a number of leisure and recreation centres established by the Umlandverband Frankfurt which offer a pleasant day in the open air, such as the Taunus Trail (Taunus-Lehrpfad) in the Saalburg-Hessenpark.

The FVV, Frankfurt's combined transport system, covers an area extending from Bad Nauheim in the north to Darmstadt in the south and from Wiesbaden in the west to Hanau in the east. Timetables are displayed at all S-Bahn, U-Bahn and tram stops. Fares are fixed on a zonal basis; the fare to a particular destination can be discovered by pressing the appropriate button on the ticket-machine.
Information about FVV services and fares: tel. 26 94-1.
Information about municipal trams, U-Bahn and buses: tel. 13 68-22 36/-22 95/-24 28.
Information about S-Bahn and railway buses: tel. 23 03 33/ 23 03 21.
Information about mail buses: tel. 28 52 40.

FVV (Frankfurter Verkehrs- und Tarifverbund)

Day trips in special trains are listed in a brochure, "Der Schöne Tag", produced by the Bundesbahn-Generalvertretung, Post-strasse 6, tel. 2 65-57 54.
Information about these trips can be obtained at railway ticket offices and DER (Deutsches Reisebüro) agencies.
For information about trips on railway buses apply to the DB-Bahnbusverkehrsstelle in the Central Station, tel. 2 65-35 87/ -54 81.

German Federal Railways (DB, Deutsche Bundesbahn)

Trips into the Taunus hills, the Rhine Valley and some of the interesting medieval towns rather farther away from Frankfurt, such as Rüdesheim, Heidelberg and Rothenburg ob der Tauber, are organised by a number of agencies: e.g. Reisebüro Wagons-Lits, Kaiserstrasse 72, tel. 26 87-2 14, Deutsche Touring GmbH, Am Römerhof 17, tel. 79 03-1, DEMA Reisen GmbH, Tour Center, Karlsruher Strasse 18, tel. 23 13 22/23.

Coach trips

The Casino Express is a coach service to the casinos at Bad Homburg or Wiesbaden. No fare is charged on the coach: the cost is included in the admission charge or can be paid in casino tokens.
Departures to Bad Homburg daily from Baseler Platz at 2.15 p.m. and thereafter every hour on the hour until 11 p.m., with the last departure at 0.45 a.m. Departures from Savignystrasse (Savigny Hotel) are 2 minutes later, from the Trade Fair Grounds (Frankfurt Plaza Hotel) 5 minutes later.

Casino Express

Practical Information

Return from Bad Homburg every hour from 3 p.m. to midnight and after the end of play between 2 and 3 a.m.
Departures to Wiesbaden daily from Baseler Platz and Central Station (south side, corner of Karlsruher Strasse) every two hours from 2 to 10 p.m., with the last departure at 0.20 a.m. From Savignystrasse (Esso petrol station) 2 minutes later, from the Messegebade (Trade Fair) Grounds (Frankfurt Plaza Hotel) 5 minutes later.
Return from Wiesbaden every two hours from 3 to 9 p.m., then at 11.30 p.m., 2 a.m. and (on Saturdays) 3 a.m.

Trips in steam trains

The Historische Eisenbahn (Historic Railway) company runs trips in trains drawn by a 40-year-old steam-engine, starting from the Mainkai at the Iron Bridge and going either westward to Frankfurt-Griesheim or eastward to Frankfurt-Mainkur. Information from Historische Eisenbahn Frankfurt, Eschborner Landstrasse 140, tel. 53 91 47.

Boat trips on the Main and Rhine

Trips are run by the Wikinger line (tel. 35 54 67 / 29 39 60) and Primus line (tel. 28 18 84 / 28 28 84), both at Mainkai 36. Departures from the Iron Bridge for round trips on the Main or excursions upstream to Seligenstadt or downstream to the Rhine. Information about timetables and fares can be obtained by telephoning the numbers given above or from the ticket office at the Iron Bridge.

Köln-Düsseldorfer (KD German Rhine Line)

The Köln-Düsseldorfer line runs excursions to the Rhine on the hydrofoil "Rheinpfiel" and other vessels. It also offers combined rail and boat trips and boat trips with a sightseeing flight over the Rhine Valley. Departures from the Iron Bridge. Information from the Köln-Dusseldorfer office (tel. 28 24 20) at the Iron Bridge or from the ticket office.

Fairs and popular festivals

February

Shrovetide Fair on Römerberg.
Parade through the city centre on Sunday of Shrovetide.
Heddernheim Shrovetide parade on Shrove Tuesday.

April

Dippemess at Ratsweg fairground (a traditional spring fair, originally a pottery market).

May/June

Wäldchestag, on Tuesday after Whitsun: the great Frankfurt festival, celebrated in the Wäldchen (Little Forest) at the Oberforsthaus, the Head Forester's house.

July

Höchst Castle Festival.

July/August

Main Festival on Römerberg and Mainkai, with the traditional Fischerstechen (a contest in which two men standing in boats try to knock one another into the water with long poles).

August

Bergen Market (cattle show).
Open Day: Römerberg, Town Hall and other municipal premises open to the public, with popular festival.
Autumn Dippemess.

October

Six-Day Race in Festhalle, Trade Fair Grounds.

Christmas Fair on Römerberg and Paulsplatz.
Christmas-Tree Fair at Iron Bridge.

Galleries

In addition to the large municipal galleries and museums, in which the works on display are not for sale, there are numerous private galleries offering works of art of varying degrees of quality and at varying cost.
The addresses of private galleries and art-dealers can be found in the "yellow pages" (gelbe Seiten) telephone directory under the headings "Antiquariate", "Antiquitäten", "Bilder und Bilderrahmen" and "Kunsthandlungen".

Hotels

A list of hotels and pensions (guest-houses) can be obtained from the Frankfurt Tourist Information Office: Frankfurter Verkehrsverein, Gutleutstrasse 7–9, D-6000 Frankfurt am Main 1.

List of hotels
(Hotelverzeichnis)

Hotel rooms can be booked through the following agencies:

Accommodation service
(Zimmervermittlung)

Frankfurter Verkehrsverein
Tourist Information in Central Station (north side, opposite platform 23), tel. 23 10 55/23 22 18 (accommodation service and information)
Open weekdays 8 a.m. to 9/10 p.m., Sun. and public holiday 9.30 a.m.–8 p.m.
Hauptwache U-Bahn station (in arcade), tel. 28 74 86
Open Mon.–Fri. 9 a.m.–6 p.m., Sat. 9 a.m.–2 p.m.

DER (Deutsches Reisebüro)
Airport, Arrival area B 6, tel. 69 30 71
Open daily 8 a.m.–9 p.m.

FAG Reisebüro, Airport, Arrival area B, tel. 6 90–25 95/-26 68
Open daily 8 a.m.–9 p.m.

Trade Fair
Ludwig-Erhard-Anlage 1, tel. 75 75-2 22/-2 89
Hall 1 (Fair participants only)
Open Mon.–Fri. 8 a.m.–4 p.m., during fairs daily 8 a.m.–9 p.m.

*Steigenberger Hotel Frankfurter Hof, Am Kaiserplatz 17, 600 beds, restaurants
Hotel am Anlagenring, Eschenheimer Anlage 23, 45 beds
Hotel am Dom, Kannengiessergasse 3, 60 beds, no restaurant
Frankfurt Scala Hotel, Schäfergasse 31, 100 beds, restaurant
Hotel Plaza, Schillerstrasse 42–44, 90 beds, restaurant
Hotel Rex, Berliner Strasse 31, 58 beds, restaurant
Hotel Schwille, Grosse Bockenheimer Strasse 50, 90 beds, restaurant
Turm-Hotel, Eschersheimer Landstrasse 20, 130 beds, restaurant
Weisses Haus, Jahnstrasse 18, 53 beds, restaurant

Hotels in central area

Practical Information

	Hotel Zentrum-Hauptwache, Rossmarkt 7, 60 beds, no restaurant
Near Central Station	°Hotel Frankfurt Intercontinental, Wilhelm-Leuschner-Strasse 43, 1500 beds, indoor swimming-pool, sauna, restaurants
	Parkhotel Frankfurt, Wiesenhüttenplatz 28–38, 400 beds, sauna, restaurant
	Frankfurt Savoy-Hotel, Wiesenhüttenstrasse 42, 200 beds, restaurant, sauna
	Hotel Ambassador, Moselstrasse 12, 120 beds, restaurant
	Hotel Excelsior Monopol, Mannheimer Strasse 7–13, 500 beds, restaurant
	Hotel Kaiserhof, Kaiserstrasse 62, 71 beds, no restaurant
	Hotel Münchner Hof, Münchener Strasse 46, 72 beds, restaurant
	Hotel National, Baseler Strasse 50, 130 beds, restaurant
	Hotel Palace, Mainluststasse 17, 84 beds, restaurant
	Hotel Ravel, Niddastrasse 39, 48 beds, restaurant
	Württemberger Hof, Karlstrasse 14, 100 beds, restaurant
Westend and near Trade Fair	°Hessischer Hof, Friedrich-Ebert-Anlage 40, 200 beds, restaurant
	°Canadian Pacific Frankfurt Plaza Hotel, Hamburger Allee 2–10, 1182 beds, sauna, restaurant
	Savigny-Hotel, Savignystrasse 14–16, 150 beds, restaurant
	Hotel Palmengarten, Palmengartenstrasse 8, 28 beds, no restaurant
	Hotel an der Messe, Westendstrasse 102, 88 beds, no restaurant
On south side of Main	Arabella Hotel Frankfurt, Lyoner Strasse 44–48, 600 beds, restaurant, sauna
	Holiday Inn Frankfurt City Tower, Mailänder Strasse 1, 328 beds, restaurant
	Crest Hotel Frankfurt, Isenburger Schneise 40, 439 beds, restaurant
	Hotel Maingau, Schifferstrasse 38–40, 140 beds, restaurant
At Airport	°Frankfurt Sheraton Hotel, Terminal Mitte (Central), 1100 beds, indoor swimming-pool, sauna, restaurant
	°Steigenberger Airporthotel, Flughafenstrasse 300–304, 500 beds, indoor swimming-pool, sauna, restaurant

Information

Römertelefon	The Römertelefon (information bureau) answers queries of all kinds. Römerberg 32, tel. 2 12-40 00/-41 00. Open Mon.–Fri. 8 a.m.–4.30 p.m., Sat. 8 a.m.–midday.
Jugend-Kiosk (Youth Kiosk)	Information centre for young people: advertisement board, leaflets and brochures, programmes, list of youth hostels, tickets for young people's concerts. Hauptwache, level B. Open Mon.–Fri. 2–6.30 p.m.
Amt für Fremdenverkehr (Office of Tourism)	This office advises on the organisation of conferences and congresses, prepares programmes of all kinds and arranges for interpreters, etc. if required. Gutleutstrasse 7–9, tel. 2 12–36 77.
Frankfurter Verkehrsverein (Tourist Information Office)	Tourist Information, Central Station (north side, opposite platform 23), tel. 23 10 55/23 22 18. Open 1 November–

31 March, daily 8 a.m.–9 p.m., Sundays and public holidays midday–8 p.m.; 1 April–31 October, daily 8 a.m.–10 p.m., Sundays and public holidays 9.30 a.m.–8 p.m.
Information Bureau, Hauptwache, Level B, tel. 28 74 86.
Accommodation service. Open weekdays 9 a.m.–6 p.m., Saturdays 9 a.m.–2 p.m.

For information (in English and French as well as German) about trams, U-Bahn and buses in Frankfurt and surrounding area, tel. 13 68-22 36/-22 95/-24 28.

Stadtwerke
(municipal transport)

For information about trains (S-Bahn) and railway buses in Frankfurt and surrounding area, tel. 23 03 33/23 03 21.

Deutsche Bundesbahn
(Federal Railways)

Jazz spots

See below, Music

Libraries and archives

Staufenstrasse 1
Open: Mon.–Fri. midday–6 p.m.
Trams: 12, 17, 21, 22 (Opernplatz)
Some 30,000 volumes by American authors. Music department with 3000 American records.

America House Library
(Amerika-Haus-Bibliothek)

Wiesbadener Strasse; entrance Römerhof 36
Open: Mon.–Thu. 8 a.m.–4.30 p.m., Fri. 8 a.m.–1 p.m.
Buses: 33, 34 (Opel-Rondell)

Battelle Institute Library
(Bibliothek des Battelle-Instituts)

Evangelischer Gemeindeverband,
Römerberg 9
Open (lending department and reading room): Mon., Wed. and Thu. 9 a.m.–midday and 2–6 p.m., Tue. 2–6 p.m., Fri. 9 a.m.–midday
Trams: 13, 14, 15, 16, 18 (Rathaus/Paulskirche)

Central Theological Library
(Theologische Zentralbücherei)

Börsenplatz
Open (lending department and reading room): Mon.–Fri. 9 a.m.–3 p.m.
Tram: 12 (Schillerstrasse)

Chamber of Commerce and Industry Library
(Bibliothek der Industrie- und Handelskammer)

Privatsammlung (Private Collection) Wilhelm Staudinger, Frankfurt-Eschersheim, Klarastrasse 5
Open: Fri. 5–7 p.m. (or by arrangement: tel. 52 48 90)
U-Bahn: U 1–3 (Lindenbaum)

Chaplin Archives
(Chaplin-Archiv)

Aussenstelle Frankfurt (Frankfurt Section),
Seckbächer Gasse 4
Open: Mon.–Thu. 8 a.m.–1 p.m. and 2–4 p.m., Fri. 8 a.m.–4 p.m.
Trams: 13, 14, 15, 16, 17, 18, 21, 22 (Theaterplatz)
U-Bahn: U 1–4 (Theaterplatz)
Archives of the Imperial Supreme Court (Reichskammergericht), the German Confederation (1815–66) and the German National Assembly.

Federal Archives
(Bundesarchiv)

Practical Information

Film Archives
(Archiv für Filmkunde)

Klarastrasse 5
Admission by appointment only
U-Bahn: U 1–3 (Lindenbaum)

Free German Foundation
Library
(Bibliothek des Freien
Deutschen Hochstiftes)

Grosser Hirschgraben 23
Open: Mon.–Fri. 10 a.m.–midday and 1–4 p.m.
S-Bahn: S 1–6 (Hauptwache)
U-Bahn: U 1–3 (Hauptwache)
Trams: 17, 21, 22 (Goetheplatz)
Reference library with reading room: 100,000 volumes and
20,000 manuscripts on the literature of the Goethe period and
Romanticism.

French Institute Library
(Institut Français)

Am Leonhardsbrunn 4
Open: Mon.–Fri. 3–7 p.m.
Buses: 32, 33 (Ditmarstrasse)
A lending and reference library.

German Institute of
International Educational
Research
(Deutsches Institut für
Internationale Pädagogische
Forschung)

Schloss-strasse 29
Open: reading room Mon.–Thu. 9 a.m.–midday and 1–5 p.m.,
Fri. 9 a.m.–midday and 1–4.30 p.m.; lending department
Mon.–Fri. 10 a.m.–midday and 2–6 p.m.
Trams: 18, 21, 22 (Kurfürstenplatz)

German Library
(Deutsche Bibliothek)

Zeppelinalle 8 (new building planned)
Open: reading room Mon.–Fri. 9 a.m.–8 p.m., Sat. 9 a.m.–
5 p.m.; catalogues Mon.–Fri. 9 a.m.–7 p.m., Sat. 11 a.m.–1 p.m.
Trams: 17, 19, 21, 22 (Bockenheimer Warte)
Reference library: all books published in Germany and all
German-language books published abroad since 1945. The
bibliographical centre and National Library of the German
Federal Republic.

German Resistance Archives
(Dokumentationsarchiv des
Deutschen Widerstandes)

Rossertstrasse 9
Open: Tue.–Thu. 10 a.m.–5 p.m.
Trams: 17, 19, 21, 22 (Siesmayerstrasse)
Archives of the Centre for the Study of the German Resistance
(1933–45).

Gmelin Institute Library
(Bibliothek des Gmelin-
Instituts)

Varrentrappstrasse 40–42
(Books borrowed through Senckenberg Library, see entry for
opening times)
A scientific library specialising in inorganic chemistry. Associated with it are the Nuclear Energy Documentation Centre
and the research centre of the Max Planck Society.

Hindemith Archives
(Paul-Hindemith-Archiv)

Rokthschildpalais,
Untermainkai 14–15
Open: Tue.–Sun. 10 a.m.–5 p.m., Wed. 10 a.m.–8 p.m.
Trams: 17, 21, 22 (Theaterplatz)

Historical Museum Library
(Bibliothek des Historischen
Museums

Saalgasse 19
Open: Tue.–Fri. 10 a.m.–midday and 2–5 p.m.
Trams: 13, 14, 15, 16, 18 (Rathaus/Paulskirche)

Municipal Archives
(Stadtarchiv)

Karmelitergasse 5
Open: Mon.–Fri. 8 a.m.–4 p.m.
Trams: 13, 14, 15, 16, 17, 18, 21, 22 (Theaterplatz)
The oldest and one of the three largest collections of municipal

archives in the Federal Republic; records and documents on the history of Frankfurt going back to the 9th c.

Zeil 17–19 (Central Library)
U-Bahn: U 4, U 5 (Konstablerwache)
Information, general non-fiction: tel. 2 12-55 79
Information, literature and foreign languages: tel. 2 12-83 53
Open: Tue.–Fri. 10 a.m.–7 p.m., Sat. 10 a.m.–1 p.m.
Central Children's Library
Open: Tue.–Fri. midday–6 p.m., Sat. 10 a.m.–1 p.m.
Music Library
Open: Tue.–Fri. 10 a.m.–6 p.m., Sat. 10 a.m.–1 p.m.
Record Library
Open: Tue.–Fri. 1–7 p.m., Sat. 10 a.m.–1 p.m.
There are also 19 branch libraries and a mobile library which visits 30 areas every week. Addresses and opening times: tel. 2 12-45 10.

Municipal Library (Stadtbücherei)

Bockenheimer Landstrasse 134–138
Open: Mon.–Fri. 8.30 a.m.–8 p.m., Sat. 9 a.m.–6 p.m. (main reading room)
Lending department: Mon., Wed. and Fri. 10 a.m.–4.30 p.m., Tue. and Thu. 10 a.m.–8 p.m.
Information: Mon.–Fri. 8.30 a.m.–7 p.m., Sat. 9 a.m.–1 p.m.
Trams: 17, 19, 21, 22 (Bockenheimer Warte)
Scholarly and scientific literature for study, education, professional interests and hobbies. Books lent, as in all Frankfurt lending libraries, free of charge. Special section on Frankfurt. Music Department (Mauskopf Museum on the History of Music). Schopenhauer Archives.

Municipal and University Library (Stadt- und Universitätsbibliothek)

Waldschmidtstrasse 43
Open: Mon. and Thu. 1–7 p.m., Tue., Wed. and Fri. 1–5 p.m.
Tram: 15 (Waldschmidtstrasse)

Pfungst Foundation Library (Technische Bibliothek der Dr.-Arthur-Pfungst Foundation)

Mementoes of the philosopher and his library of 600 volumes. A special section of the Municipal and University Library (see above).

Schopenhauer Archives (Schopenhauer-Archiv)

Saalgasse 15
Open: Mon., Wed. and Thu. 8 a.m.–4 p.m., Tue. 8 a.m.–6p.m., Fri. 8.30 a.m.–4 p.m.
U-Bahn: U 4 (Römer)

Schweitzer Archives (Albert-Schweitzer-Archiv)

Bockenheimer Landstrasse 136–138
Open: Mon.–Fri. 8.30 a.m.–8 p.m., Sat. 9 a.m.–1 p.m.
Trams: 17, 19, 21, 22 (Bockenheimer Warte)
A specialised natural history library.

Senckenberg Library (Senckenbergische Bibliothek)

Schaumainkai 63
Open: Tue.–Sat. 10 a.m.–5 p.m.
Buses: 46, 961, 963, 972, 973 (Untermainbrücke)
Reference library on the history of art.

Städel Institute Library (Kunsthistorische Bibliothek des Städelschen Kunstinstitutes)

Theodor-Stern-Kai 7
Open: Mon., Thu. and Fri 10 a.m.–5 p.m., Tue. and Wed. 10 a.m.–8 p.m.
Tram: 21 (Klinikum)
Medicine and the history of medicine.

University Clinic Library (Hauptbibliothek des Klinikums der Johann-Wolfgang-Goethe-Universität)

Lost property offices

Städtisches Fundbüro (Municipal Lost Property Office), Mainzer Landstrasse 323
Open: Mon.–Fri. 7.30 a.m.–1 p.m.
Property found on the streets and in municipal establishments

Flughafen-Fundbüro (Airport Lost Property Office), Arrival area A
Open: daily 7 a.m.–7 p.m., after that at Left Luggage office
Property found in the Airport

Fundstelle der Deutschen Bundesbahn (Railway Lost Property Office),
Central Station (north side, platform 24)
Open: 24 hours a day
Offices and store at Mannheimer Strasse 2
Property found on S-Bahn and Federal Railways

Fundbüro der Stadtwerke (Municipal Transport Lost Property Office), Hauptwache U-Bahn Station (in arcade)
Open: Mon.–Fri. 7 a.m.–6 p.m.
Property found in municipal buses, trams and U-Bahn

Markets

Covered markets

While the produce displayed in the Central Market (see entry), which handles fruit and vegetables from the whole Rhine-Main area, is sold only to dealers, the Little Market Hall (see entry) in Hasengasse attracts ordinary customers with a tempting variety of crisp vegetables and fresh herbs, appetising fruit, crusty bread and an enormous range of cheeses. And this piece of anticipated culinary delights has recently acquired an additional attraction in the Turkish butchers now installed on the upper floor, offering savoury wares which bring a breath of the East.

Weekly markets

Friedberger Landstrasse
Mon.–Fri. 8 a.m.–6 p.m., Sat. 8 a.m.–2 p.m.
Tram: 12 (Rohrbachstrasse / Friedberger Landstrasse)

Höchst, Little Market Hall (Kleinmarkthalle)
Tue., Fri. and Sat. 8 a.m.–1 p.m.
S-Bahn: S 3 (Bahnhof Höchst)

Bornheim, Berger Strasse
Wed. 8 a.m.–6 p.m., Sat. 8 a.m.–2 p.m.
U-Bahn: U 4 (Bornheim Mitte)
Bus: 38 (Saalburgstrasse)

Motoring assistance

Motoring organisations

ADAC (Allgemeiner Deutscher Automobil-Club)
Schumannstrasse 4–6, tel. 74 30-1
Münchner Strasse 1, tel. 23 13 33
Walter-Kolb-Strasse 9–11, tel. 62 20 03

Wiesbadener Strasse (Frankfurt-West motorway exit), tel. 74 30-2 46

AvD (Automobilclub von Deutschland)
Lyoner Strasse 16, tel. 6 60 60
Information, hotel booking, money changing
Information by telephone: 6 60-63 00

ACE (Auto Club Europa)
Wilhelm-Leuschner-Strasse 69, tel. 23 51 58

ADAC: tel. 74 30-6   Breakdown service
AvD: 6 66-16 66
ACE: 23 29 29

See list in the "yellow pages" (gelbe Seiten) of the local   Repair garages
telephone directory.

Texaco tourist pilots can be found in front of the Römer and at   Pilot service
the ADAC information centre at Frankfurt-West. They provide
visiting motorists with information and pilot service free of
charge during the main holiday season in July and August.

See Radio and television (below)   Traffic information by radio

---

Museums

For most museums there are no admission fees, but a few make   Charges
charges, which are usually quite small, with reductions for
children, students and groups. Information about charges can
be obtained from the Römertelefon (2 12-40 00/-41 00).

Unless otherwise indicated, Frankfurt museums are open on   Opening times
Tuesdays and Thursdays from 10 a.m. to 5 p.m. and
Wednesdays from 10 a.m. to 8 p.m. They are usually closed on
Mondays.

Applied Arts, Museum of
See entry, A to Z

Bergen-Enkheim Local Museum (Heimatmuseum)
See entry, A to Z

Brewing Museum
See A to Z, Henninger Tower

Carmelite Friary
See entry, A to Z

Chaplin Archives
See Libraries and archives (above)

Children's Museum in Historical Museum
Saalgasse 19
Open: Tue.–Sun. 10 a.m.–5 p.m., Wed. to 8 p.m.
U-Bahn: U 4 (Römer)

Communal Gallery
See A to Z, Deutschordenshaus

Ethnology, Museum of
See entry, A to Z

Federal Postal Museum
See entry, A to Z

German Film Museum
See entry, A to Z

German Leather Museum
See entry, A to Z

German Museum of Architecture
See entry, A to Z

Goethe House
See entry, A to Z

Goethe Museum
See entry, A to Z

Heinrich Hoffmann Museum
Schubertstrasse 20
Open: Tue.–Sun. 10 a.m.–5 p.m.
Trams: 17, 19, 21, 22 (Siesmayerstrasse/Mendelssohnstrasse)

Historical Museum and Coin Cabinet
See entry, A to Z

Höchst Museum of Local History
See A to Z, Höchst, Castle

Hoechst Farbwerke Museum
See A to Z, Höchst, Castle

Liebieghaus
See entry, A to Z

Prehistory and Early History, Museum of
See A to Z, Holzhausenschlösschen

Rothschildpalais
See entry, A to Z

Schwanheim Local Museum (Heimatmuseum)
Alt Schwanheim 6
Open: Sun. 10 a.m.–midday

Sculpture, Museum of
See A to Z, Liebieghaus

Senckenberg Museum of Natural History
See entry, A to Z

Städel Art Institute and Municipal Gallery
See entry, A to Z

Stoltze Tower (Friedrich Stoltze Memorial)
Töngesgasse 34–36
Open: Mon., Tue., Thu. and Fri. 10 a.m.–5 p.m., Wed. 10 a.m.–
8 p.m.
U-Bahn: U 4 (Konstablerwache)

Struwwelpeter Museum
Hochstrasse 47
Open: Tue.–Sun. 11 a.m.–5 p.m., Wed. to 8 p.m.

Music

Central to Frankfurt's musical life are the operatic productions
of the municipal Opera House, which have won high critical
acclaim, and a wide range of orchestral concerts and solo
recitals. In addition the city has long been a stronghold of jazz.

There are seven large concert halls, mainly devoted to classical
music:

Concert halls

Old Opera House
See entry, A to Z

Jahrhunderthalle (Farbwerke Hoechst)
Silostrasse/Pfaffenwiese
Buses: 50, 51, 54 (Jahrhunderthalle)

Kongresshalle (Trade Fair Grounds)
Ludwig-Erhard-Anlage 1
Trams: 16, 18 (Festhalle/Messegelände)

Palmengarten
Siesmayerstrasse or Palmengartenstrasse
Trams: 17, 19, 21, 22 (Palmengarten)

Municipal Opera House
Theaterplatz
Trams: 13, 14, 15, 16, 17, 18, 21, 22 (Theaterplatz)
U-Bahn: U 1–4 (Theaterplatz)

Sendesaal des Hessischen Rundfunks (Studio of Hessen
Radio)
Bertramstrasse 8
U-Bahn 1–3 (Dornbusch)

Konzertsaal der Deutschen Bank
Junghofstrasse 5–11
Trams: 17, 21, 22 (Goetheplatz)

Opera and concert programmes are given daily in the local
Press ("Frankfurter Allgemeine Zeitung", "Rundschau"), also
in the twice-monthly "Frankfurter Wochenschau" and in the
monthly programmes and magazines which are available in
hotels and from kiosks. Tickets can be bought at the ticket
agencies listed in a later section (Ticket agencies, see below).

Programmes, tickets

The Frankfurt Opera has gained an international reputation
for its unconventional interpretations of well-known and

Opera

frequently performed works and its adventurous new productions of less familiar operas. Performances are given in the Opera House in Theaterplatz and not in the rebuilt Old Opera, now used only as a concert hall and congress centre. The current programme can be obtained from the Opera House (Theatres, see below), and is also given in the Press and the twice-monthly "Frankfurter Wochenschau".

Jazz

Jazz established itself in Frankfurt in the early post-war years and soon made the city one of the leading centres of jazz in Germany. There are now numerous clubs and cellars devoted to jazz, rock, folk and pop music, and during the summer many jazz musicians put on open-air performances.

Jazz spots

Jazzkeller
Modern, hot and free jazz
Kleine Bockenheimer Strasse 18a/Goethestrasse
Trams: 12, 17, 21, 22 (Opernplatz)

Jazzkneipe
Swing
Berliner Strasse 70
Trams: 13, 14, 15, 16, 18 (Rathaus/Paulskirche)

Jazz-Life-Podium
Dixieland and swing
Kleine Rittergasse 22–26, Sachsenhausen
Trams: 11, 16 (Frankensteiner Platz)

Sinkkasten
Rock jazz, blues, fringe groups
Brönnerstrasse 5
Tram: 12 (Stephanstrasse)

Jazz im Schlachthof
Old-time, Dixieland, swing, rock
Sundays from 11 a.m.
Deutschherrnufer 36, Sachsenhausen
Trams: 11, 16 (Frankensteiner Platz)

Niddapark-Terrassen
New Orleans to Country and Western
Woogstrasse 52
Trams: 18, 21 (Praunheim/Brücke)

River-Jazzkeller
Old-time to modern
Kranengasse 2, Höchst
S-Bahn: S 3 (Bahnhof Höchst)

Jazzhaus-Discographie
Kleine Bockenheimer Strasse 12
Trams: 12, 17, 21, 22 (Opernplatz)

Jazz im Palmengarten
May–September, alternate Thursdays from 7.30 p.m.
Palmengartenstrasse
Trams: 17, 19, 21, 22 (Palmengarten)

Newspapers

The "Frankfurter Allgemeine Zeitung" ("FAZ" for short) is one of West Germany's leading newspapers. It follows a conservative line, and contains much local news.

"Frankfurter Allgemeine Zeitung"

The "Frankfurter Rundschau", on the liberal left, specialises in local and regional news.

"Frankfurter Rundschau"

The middle-of-the-road "Frankfurter Neue Presse" is also strong on regional news.

"Frankfurter Neue Presse"

The popular Press is represented by the "Abendpost' night edition, the "Frankfurter Rundschau am Abend" and "BILD-Frankfurt".

Popular papers

There are also a number of local advertising papers including "Blitz-Tip" and the "Frankfurter Nachrichten" which are distributed free to households in the district and are read more for their small ads than their local news.

Advertising papers

Night life

Frankfurt's night life has earned the city a dubious fame as the hottest spot in Germany. Particularly around the Central Station it flourishes in a concentration and lack of inhibition unequalled in any other German city with the exception of

Night spots in the neighbourhood of the Central Station

Hamburg. Those interested in this form of entertainment will not need to consult any guide to help them to track down their particular preferences. In this section we list only a few of the better class of establishment.

Closing hours vary. Many places close at 1 a.m., others at 2 a.m., others again – particularly when there is a trade fair on – at 4 in the morning.

Discothèques

St John's Inn
Grosser Hirschgraben 20 (opposite the Goethe House)
Open: Mon.–Sat. 8 p.m.–2 a.m., closed Sun.
Admission subject to management approval

Vogue
Junghofstrasse 14
Open: Mon.–Sat. 10 a.m.–4 a.m., closed Sun. (except during trade fairs)

Tangente
Bockenheimer Landstrasse 87
Open: daily 10 p.m.–4 a.m.
Club card or "personality" requisite

Dorian Gray
Airport, Area C, Level 0
Open: daily 9 p.m.–6 a.m.
The haunt of the jet set, and so only for people with "personality"

Hotel bars

Blue Infinitum
(Hotel Frankfurt Plaza)
Hamburger Allee 2
Open: daily 9.30 p.m.–4 a.m.

Montgolfière
(Steigenberger Airporthotel)
Flughafenstrasse 300–304
Open: daily 9 p.m.–2 a.m.

Jimmy's Bar
(Hotel Hessischer Hof)
Friedrich-Ebert-Anlage 40
Open: daily 8 p.m.–4 a.m.

Casablanca Bar
(Parkhotel)
Wiesenhüttenplatz 38
Open: daily 6.30–11 p.m.

Opening times

Department stores

Mon.–Fri. 8.30 a.m.–6.30 p.m., Sat. 8.30 a.m.–2 p.m.; first Saturday in month 8.30 a.m.–6 p.m.

Other shops

Individual opening times vary within statutory limits: opening between 7 and 9 a.m. (bakers and newsagents at 7 a.m.), usually closing for lunch from 1 to 3 (except many shops in the city centre) and closing in the evening at 6 or 6.30.

It is left to individual shops to decide whether to stay open on "long Saturday" (the first Saturday in the month); outside the city centre most shops close at 2 p.m.

All shops are closed on Church festivals and public holidays, and also on the afternoon of Shrove Tuesday and the afternoon of Wäldchestag (see Fairs and popular festivals) from 1 p.m.

Public holidays

Urgent requirements can be bought in the shopping arcade at the Central Station (see entry) and at the Airport (see entry) until about 8.30 p.m.

After-hours shopping

See separate entries

Post offices
Museums
Banks

Post offices

Post offices in the city are open Mon.–Fri. 8 a.m.–6 p.m., Sat. 8 a.m.–midday. The post offices in the Central Station and at the Airport are open 24 hours a day. The Head Post Office is open daily from 7 a.m. to 9.30 p.m., though with restricted services outside normal opening hours.

Opening times

Head Post Office (Hauptpost), Zeil 110, tel. 2 11-1
Airport Post Office (Flughafen-Postamt), 6000 Frankfurt 75, tel. 69 76-1

Poste restante

Money can be changed at the Head Post Office and the Airport Post Office.

Changing money

Public holidays

The following public holidays (on which shops are closed) are observed in Frankfurt:
New Year's Day (1 January); Shrove Tuesday (afternoon); Good Friday, Easter Day and Easter Monday; 1 May; Ascension; Whit Sunday and Whit Monday; Wäldchestag (Tuesday after Whitsun, afternoon); Corpus Christi; German Unity Day (17 June); Day of Prayer and Repentance; Christmas Eve (24 December, afternoon), Christmas Day and 26 December; New Year's Eve (31 December, afternoon).

Public transport

The abbreviation FVV stands for Frankfurter Verkehrs- und Tarifverbund (Transport and Tariff Combine), which takes in the S-Bahn, U-Bahn, buses and trams. The same tickets (which must be obtained from the blue ticket machines at stations and stops) are used in all forms of transport.

FVV

The city and surrounding area are divided into three tariff zones, shown on the FVV route plans in different colours. To discover the fare to a particular destination, note the colour of the zone in which it lies and press the button of that colour on the ticket

Fares

machine. The machine accepts 10 and 50 pfennig and 1 and 2 mark coins. A ticket is valid for an hour, and must be shown to an inspector on request.

Travelling without a ticket is not to be recommended: if you are caught there is a fine of 40 DM.

A 24-hour ticket is a good bargain for visitors. It costs about the same as four individual tickets and allows unrestricted travel for 24 hours on public transport within the city (i.e. in tariff zone 1).

Children's fares

Children under 15 pay half fare (press the "Children" button on the ticket machine); children under 6 accompanied by an adult travel free.

Rush hour travel

During the morning and evening rush hours (Mondays to Fridays 6.30–8 a.m. and 4–6.30 p.m.) the ordinary price ticket is increased by 20 per cent.

Information

FVV tariff:
Mannheimer Strasse 15–19, tel. 26 94-1

Timetables of trams, U-Bahn and municipal buses (two-figure numbers): tel. 13 68-22 36/-22 95/-24 28

Timetables of S-Bahn and railway (DB) buses (three-figure numbers): tel. 23 03 33 / 23 03 21

Timetables of mail buses (DBP):
tel. 28 52 40

Radio and television

The Frankfurt area is served by the Hessen Radio Corporation (Hessischer Rundfunk), whose headquarters and studios are at Bertramstrasse 8 (see A to Z, Hessen Radio). Concerts are given in the main studio in the Funkhaus (Radio House), Am Dornbusch, and also in the studios in Bertramstrasse.

Radio

There are three radio programmes, hr 1, 2 and 3.

The first programme, hr 1, is popular in tone, with light music, news stories and commentaries, and news bulletins every hour on the hour.

The second programme, hr 2, is cultural and educational in content, with talks, plays and serious music.

The third programme, hr 3, transmits news, traffic announcements, guidance for motorists and information, interspersed with light music. In the evening there are foreign-language transmissions intended for foreigners working in Germany.

hr 1

News and weather reports:
Mon.-Fri. 6, 7 and 7.30 a.m., 8 a.m.–7 p.m. and 10 p.m.–midnight on the hour
Sat. as for Mon.–Fri. except 4 and 5 p.m.
Sun. hourly from 6–10 a.m., noon–3 p.m., 6 and 7 p.m. and 10 p.m.–midnight

"Rundschau aus dem Hessenland' (magazine programme): daily at 12.50 and 6.50 p.m.

Stock Exchange report: Mon.–Fri. at 2.50 p.m.
Sports round-up: Wed. at 10.20 p.m.

Music, cultural programmes, school programmes, radio plays,   hr 2
social and political programmes

News every hour on the hour; travel and service information at   hr 3
least every half hour

Weather reports for travellers (and from 30 November winter
sports reports): Mon.–Sat. at 10.45 a.m., Sun. at 2.30 p.m.

What's on: Mon.–Fri. at 11.45 a.m., Sat. at 2.45 p.m.

Hessen Radio is part of the national network of the Federal   Television
Republic, and transmits all networked programmes, while
making its own contributions to the network, such as the
"Magazin der Woche" ("Magazine of the Week") programme.

Restaurants

For hotel restaurants, see Hotels, above

Bräustüberl,   Frankfurt cuisine
Fahrtor 1

Altes Zollhaus,
Friedberger Landstrasse 531

Zur Müllerin,
Weissfrauenstrasse 18 /Theaterplatz

Zum Karrenberg,
Kirchnerstrasse 7 / Grosse Gallusstrasse

Heylands Weinstuben,
Kaiserhofstrasse 7 /Fressgass

Börsenkeller,
Schillerstrasse 11/Börsenplatz

Dippegucker,
Eschenheimer Anlage/Oeder Weg

Sudpfanne,
Eschersheimer Landstrasse 20

Schnecken-Pit,
Herderstrasse 2

Teehaus (Chinese),   East Asian
Fahrgasse 3/Alte Brücke

Asia (Chinese),
Gallusanlage 2

Peking (Chinese),
Kaiserstrasse 15

Lotos (Chinese),
Grosse Bockenheimer Strasse 37

Mikuni (Japanese),
Fahrgasse 93

Seoul (Korean),
Wächtersbacher Strasse 74

Sawadi (Thai),
Grosse Friedberger Strasse 34

French   Ernos Bistro,
Liebigstrasse 15/Staufenstrasse

Le Caveau,
Deutschherrnufer 29

Bistro 77,
Ziegelhüttenweg 1–3

Bistro M,
Wendelsweg 79

Maison Pierre,
Junghofstrasse 14/Alte Rothofstrasse

Baron de la Mouette
(Mövenpick),
Neue Mainzer Strasse/Opernplatz·

Jacques Offenbach,
(in basement of Old Opera House),
Opernplatz

Adloff,
Hochstrasse 27

Weinhaus Brückenkeller,
Schützenstrasse 6

Weidemann,
Kelsterbacher Strasse 69, Niederrad

Greek   Bacchus,
Waldschmidtstrasse 59 (Zoo)

Nibelungen-Schänke,
Nibelungenallee 55

Dionysos,
Rödelheimer Strasse 34/Breitenbachbrücke

Alt-Athen,
Darmstädter Landstrasse 6/Schifferstrasse

Italian   Da Bruno,
Elbestrasse 15/Münchener Strasse

Da Claudio,
Zum-Jungen-Strasse 10/Am Dornbusch

Casa del Pittore,
Zeisselstrasse 20

Pirandello,
Friedberger Landstrasse 95

Casa Nova,
Stresemannallee 38, Sachsenhausen

Da Angelo,
Reuterweg 50/Elsheimer Strasse

Golfo di Napoli,
Leipziger Strasse 16, Bockenheim

Alassio,
Bockenheimer Landstrasse 99

Atelier,
Ginnheimer Landstrasse 49

Firenze,
Berger Strasse 30

Stadt Malaga,   Spanish
Töngesgasse 11

Bodega Luciano,
Kiesstrasse 39/Adalbertstrasse, Bockenheim

Manolo,
Schwanheimer Strasse 70a, Schwanheim

Belgrad,   Yugoslav
Eckenheimer Landstrasse 127

Split,
Kleine Brückenstrasse 14, Sachsenhausen

Patrizier,
Savignystrasse 22

Rail travel

Train Information, Central Station, tel. 23 03 33, 23 03 21   Train information
DER (Deutsches Reisebüro), Central Station, tel. 23 09 11,
23 61 39

Information Bureau of Verkehrsverein, Central Station (north
side, opposite platform 23), open daily from 8 a.m. to 9 or
10 p.m., Sundays and public holidays 9.30 a.m.–8 p.m.

Tel. 23 09 11   Motorail

Tel. 2 65-56 47   Express goods – despatch

Practical Information

Express goods – collection	Tel. 2 65-51 35/-51 36/-51 38

Timetable information

Trains to and from north: tel. 1 15 31
North-east to east: 1 15 32
South-east to south: 1 15 33
South: 1 15 34
South-west: 1 15 35
West to north-west: 1 15 36
U-Bahn, trams, buses: 1 15 37
Automatic timetable information from "Karlchen" the computer: tel. 7 54 32

House-to-house luggage delivery	Tel. 23 03 33, 23 09 11
Seat reservation	Tel. 23 09 11, 23 61 39
Railway buses, S-Bahn	Tel. 23 03 33, 23 03 21
Special trains, excursions	Tel. 2 65-54 64/-38 87/-54 81

Railway stations

Central Station
(Hauptbahnhof)

Frankfurt Central Station is one of the largest railway termini in Europe, handling some 250,000 passengers and 1 500 trains on an average weekday, and an important junction for both domestic and international traffic from north to south and east to west, a station in the Intercity system and the central junction and terminus of the Frankfurt Transport Combine (FVV).

Facilities available in Central Station:
Bars, bookshops, chemist, DER (Deutsches Reisebüro) offices, Deutsche Touring office (south side, Mannheimer Strasse 4), flower shop, foodshops, hairdresser (open Mon.–Sat. 6 a.m.–9 p.m.), information office of Verkehrsverein (accommodation service; north side, opposite platform 23), lockers, lost property office, luggage despatch office, money-changing (Deutsche Verkehrs-Kredit-Bank: open daily 6.30 a.m.–10 p.m.), news cinema, newspaper kiosk (with foreign papers), post office (open day and night), Railway Mission, restaurants and snack bars.

South Station
(Südbahnhof)

Trains to Central Station, Wächtersbach, Bad Soden–Salmünster, Gelnhausen, Fulda, Hanau, Aschaffenburg and Miltenberg (the last three via Frankfurt East Station).

East Station
(Ostbahnhof)

Trains to Hanau, Aschaffenburg, Frankfurt Central and South Stations; railway buses to Dörnigheim and Hanau.

Frankfurt-Höchst

Trains to Central Station, Königstein, Wiesbaden and Niedernhausen; railway buses to Königstein and Bad Soden.

Shopping

The busiest shopping area in Frankfurt is in the Zeil and neighbouring streets, with both department stores and a great range of specialist shops, including some very high-class establishments indeed.

The shops in the shopping centres under the forecourt of the Central Station, in Bergen-Enkheim (the Hessen-Center) and at the airport are mostly open beyond the usual shop closing times.

See also Boutiques, Souvenirs

Sightseeing tours

March–October, daily 10 a.m.–2 p.m.; 1 November–15 December and 15 January–end February, daily at 2 p.m. Departure from Central Station
Duration: $2\frac{1}{2}$–3 hours
This tour takes in the Goethe House, the Römer and Imperial Hall, the Cathedral, the Paulskirche and the Palmengarten, with commentary in English as well as German.

Stadtrundfahrten Frankfurt am Main

3 January–20 December, daily at 11 a.m.; 31 January–30 November, daily at 11 a.m. and 3.15 p.m. Departure from Central Station (south side)
Duration: $2\frac{1}{2}$ hours without lunch, $3\frac{3}{4}$ hours including lunch Commentaries on headphones in various foreign languages as well as German

Stadtrundfahrt Frankfurt Vision

A sightseeing tour that is different, in a brightly painted old-time tram. This "Cider Express" leaves the East Station every half hour on Saturday and Sunday afternoons between 1 and 6 o'clock and follows a circular route via Sachsenhausen,

Ebbelwei-Express

Sightseeing on the Ebbelwei-Express

161

Theaterplatz, Opernplatz, Central Station, Paulskirche and Allerheiligentor, and so back to the station. The fare includes a bottle of *Ebbelwei* (cider) or apple juice and two pretzels. The Ebbelwei Express can also be hired for a private party.
Information: Stadtwerke, Rathenauplatz 3, tel. 13 68-24 25.

Private guided tours

The members of a voluntary organisation, Freundeskreis Liebenswertes Frankfurt (roughly translated, "Friends of Frankfurt"), take groups of visitors round the city, introducing them not only to the principal sights but also to some aspects of the city that are not on the beaten tourist track. The guides' services are given free of charge.
Enquiries: tel. 54 30 78

Tours of airport

Tours of the Rhine-Main Airport can be arranged for groups of 20 or more between 8.30 a.m. and 4.30 p.m. The tour lasts about 45 minutes and takes in the apron, runways, freight centre, etc. Explanations are in German.
Reduced charge for children under 16 and the disabled.
There are also tours (groups only; duration 2 hours; 8.30 a.m.–4.30 p.m.) of the service installations, conveyor system, maintenance sheds and tower.

Spectator terraces: see Airport (above)

Souvenirs

The best-known souvenir of Frankfurt is the *Bembel*, the typical cider jug of grey stoneware, painted in blue. The real thing, from the Westerwald pottery, can be obtained from Maurers' in Sachsenhausen (Wallstrasse 5) or, in a more traditionally Frankfurt way, at the Dippemess Fair in spring or autumn.
Another popular souvenir is Frankfurt's mascot, a figure of Struwwelpeter.
For those with a sweet tooth there are the "Bethmännchen" of Frankfurt – marzipan balls with almonds stuck into the sides.

Souvenir shops are to be found wherever tourists go – for example in the Hauptwache shopping arcade (level B), around the Central Station and in the Zeil and Römer pedestrian precincts.

Sport

Information

For information about sports facilities, clubs, etc., apply to the Römertelefon, tel. 2 12-40 00 or -41 00, or the Sport- und Badeamt, Hochstrasse 4–8, tel. 2 12-38 87.

"Trim trails"

There are eight *Trimmpfade* ("trim trails" or "keep-fit trails") in the Stadtwald (see entry A to Z) and city parks:
Fitnessplatz Grüneburgpark
Schweisstropfenbahn Waldstadion
Trimmpfad am Goetheturm
Trimmbahn Sportplatz Ginnheimer Landstrasse
Trimmpfad Riederwald

Pedestrian precinct in the city centre

Trimmpfad Tannenwald (Neu-Isenburg)
Trimmpfad Huth-Park
Trimmplatz Schwanheimer Hölle

Courts can be booked (prior application required) at the following places: Tennis

Waldstadion
Mörfelder Landstrasse 362, tel. 6 70 80 12
20 outdoor courts; other courts indoors

Europa Tennis und Squash Park
Ginnheimer Landstrasse 49, tel. 53 20 40
5 outdoor and 3 indoor courts
Open 5 a.m.–midnight

Tennisanlage Klüh
Im Uhrig 29, tel. 52 51 18
16 outdoor and 2 indoor courts

City Squash Center   Squash
Kaiserstrasse 73, tel. 23 25 27
Open Mon.–Fri. 10 a.m.–11 p.m., Sat. noon–8 p.m.
All equipment can be hired

Top Squash Club
Niddagaustrasse 7, tel. 78 50 71/72
Rackets can be hired

Squash-Zentrum Ost
Ostparkstrasse 35, tel. 43 47 56
Open daily 10 a.m.–11 p.m.

Europa Tennis und Squash Park
Ginnheimer Landstrasse 49, tel. 53 20 40
Open daily 5 a.m.–midnight

Tennispark 1880
Adickesallee, tel. 47 10 07 / 59 15 57

Ice-skating

Eissporthalle Ratsweg
Open daily 8 a.m.–10 p.m.
2 rinks and 1 speed circuit

Waldstadion
Mörfelder Landstrasse 362
Open Oct.–Mar. daily 9–11.30 a.m., 3–5.30 p.m. and
10 p.m.–midnight
Skates can be hired

Roller-skating

Eissporthalle Ratsweg
Speed circuit from April to September

Frankfurter Roll- un Eissportclub
Untermainkai, Am Nizza
2 rinks

Brentano-Bad
Rödelheimer Parkweg
1 rink

Waldspielplatz Tannenwald
Friedensallee, Neu-Isenburg
1 rink

Golf

Frankfurter Golf-Club
Golfstrasse 41, tel. 6 66 23 18
Open April–September from 7 or 8 a.m. to dusk
Admission to members of other clubs with handicap

Riding

Reitschule Bruno
Hahnstrasse 87, tel. 66 44 85
Open daily 8 a.m.–noon, Mon.–Fri. also 3–9 p.m.

Frankfurter Reit- un Fahrclub
Hahnstrasse 85, tel. 66 45 85
Open Mon.–Fri. 3–9 p.m., Tue.–Thu. also 9.30–10.30 a.m., Sat.
9–11 a.m. and 2–5 p.m., Sun. 9 a.m.–1 p.m.
Prior booking necessary

Swimming

See below, Swimming-pools

Stadiums

Frankfurter Waldstadion
Mörfelder Landstrasse 362
30,556 seats, standing for 30,600 (main pitch)
Major football matches

Eissporthalle Frankfurt, Ratsweg
Over 5000 seats
Ice-hockey matches, ice-skating championships

Sportanlage am Riederwald
(Eintracht Frankfurt)
Football stadium for 38,000 spectators

Swimming-pools

There are facilities for bathing, including a naturist beach, in the
Langener Waldsee, a lake just to the south of Frankfurt on B 44.
The Main is not suitable for bathing.

Frankfurt's open-air pools are open from mid May to mid   Open-air pools
September between 8 a.m. and 8 p.m. There are reduced
admission charges for children and young people between 5
and 18, students, soldiers and the severely disabled; children
under 5 are admitted free.

These pools, with water heated to 25 °C/77 °F, are open from   Heated open-air pools
1 April to 31 October.

Gartenhallenbad Am Rebstock   Rebstock-Bad
Buses: 33, 34 (Am Römerhof)
This new pool complex has both outdoor and indoor pools,
linked by a channel for swimmers, as well as a pool with
artificial waves, a sauna, an island and riverside beaches,
restaurants and a keep-fit ground.

There are reduced admission charges for the same categories as Indoor pools
at the open-air pools.

Taxis

Taxis can be called be dialling 23 00 01, 25 00 01 or 54 50 11
day or night (the tariffs are the same).
The telephone numbers of individual taxi ranks are listed in the
telephone directory under the heading "Taxizentrale".

Theatres

Theatre seats can be reserved by telephone, usually from   Advance booking
midday to an hour before curtain-up. Tickets can also be
bought at the Frankfurt Tourist Information Office (Verkehrsverein) and other Ticket agencies, see below (up to 11 days
before the performance; there may be a commisson charge).

Opera House (Oper)
Untermainanlage, tel. 25 62-3 35
Advance booking office: Mon.–Fri. 10 a.m.–6 p.m., Sat.
10 a.m.–2 p.m.
Telephone booking from noon
Box-office (tel. 25 62-3 34) open an hour before the
performance
Trams: 13, 14, 15, 16, 17, 18, 21, 22 (Theaterplatz)

165

Municipal Theatre (Schauspiel)
Theaterplatz
Advance booking office (tel. 25 62-4 35): Mon.–Fri. 10 a.m.–
6 p.m., Sat. 10 a.m.–2 p.m.
Box-office (tel. 25 62-4 34) open an hour before the
performance
Telephone booking from noon
Trams: 13, 14, 15, 16, 17, 18, 21, 22 (Theaterplatz)
U-Bahn: U 1–4 (Theaterplatz)

Kammerspiel
Hofstrasse 2
Advance booking office (tel. 25 62–4 35): Mon.–Fri. 10 a.m.–
6 p.m., Sat. 10 a.m.–2 p.m.
Box-office (tel. 25 62-3 95) open an hour before the
performance
Telephone booking from noon
Trams: 13, 14, 15, 16, 17, 18, 21, 22 (Theaterplatz)
U-Bahn: U 1–4 (Theaterplatz)

TAT – Theater am Turm
Eschersheimer Landstrasse 2, tel. 15 45-1 00/-1 10
Independent theatre; visiting companies
Tickets at box-office or through ticket agency
U-Bahn: U 1–3 (Eschenheimer Tor)

Fritz-Rémond-Theater im Zoo
Alfred-Brehm-Platz
Zoologischer Garten, tel. 43 51 66
Good quality light theatre
Box-office open 10.30 a.m.–8 p.m.
Trams: 13, 15 (Zoologischer Garten)

Die Komödie
Neue Mainzer Strasse 18, tel. 28 43 30
Box-office tel. 28 45 80
Light theatre
Trams: 13, 14, 15, 16, 17, 18, 21, 22 (Theaterplatz)
U-Bahn: U 1–4 (Theaterplatz)

Volkstheater Frankfurt
Grosser Hirschgraben 21, Cantate-Saal, tel. 28 58 98
Plays in Frankfurt dialect
Trams: 17, 21, 22 (Goetheplatz)

Die Maininger
Neue Rothofstrasse 26a, tel. 83 24 24, 28 02 27
Satirical cabaret – "Frankfurt Resistance Theatre"
Box-office open from 6 p.m.
Trams: 12, 17, 21, 22 (Opernplatz)

Die Schmiere
Seckbächer Gasse, tel. 28 10 66
Satirical cellar-theatre in Carmelite Friary
"The worst theatre in the world"
Trams: 13, 14, 15, 16, 17, 18, 21, 22 (Theaterplatz)
U-Bahn: U 1–4 (Theaterplatz)

A performance in the Municipal Theatre

Junge Bühne Frankfurt
Mainstrasse 2, tel. 28 80 23
Cellar-theatre
Tram: 16 (Börsenplatz/AOK)

Die Katakombe
Theater 2 am Zoo
Pfingstweidstrasse 2, tel. 28 47 50, 49 17 25
Telephone booking Mon.–Fri. 10 a.m.–1 p.m. and from 7 p.m.
Trams: 13, 15 (Zoologischer Garten)

Café-Theatre
Hamburger Allee 45, tel. 63 64 64
English-language theatre
Box-office (tel. 77 76 80) open from 6 p.m.
Tram: 18 (Varrentrappstrasse)

Theater Nordwest
Nidaforum 2, tel. 57 60 14, 57 05 96
Children's and young people's theatre
U-Bahn: U 1 (Nordweststadt)

Frankfurter Figurentheater
Untermainkai 14 (Rothschildpalais), tel. 70 41 44
Puppet theatre
Trams: 13, 14, 15, 16, 17, 18, 21, 22 (Theaterplatz)
U-Bahn: U 1–4 (Theaterplatz)

Practical Information

Puppenzentrum Frankfurt
Diemelstrasse 9, tel. 72 70 95
Children's puppet theatre
Trams: 18, 21, 22 (Schloss-strasse)

Ticket agencies

Amt für Fremdenverkehr (Office of Tourism),
Gutleutstrasse 7, tel. 28 74 86

Municipal Theatres Ticket Office,
Hauptwache U-Bahn station (Level B), tel. 28 37 38

Ludwig Schäfer,
Schweizer Strasse 28a, Sachsenhausen, tel. 62 37 79

Ticket Agency,
Sandweg 64, tel. 44 93 44

Towers (viewpoints)

Telecommunications Tower (Fernmeldeturm)	Telecommunications Tower 331 m (1086 ft) Wilhelm-Epstein-Strasse Viewing platform and cafeteria at over 200 m (650 ft), open daily from 9 a.m. to 10 p.m. in summer (1 April to 30 September). Reduced admission charges for children, students and parties.
Tower of Cathedral (Domturm)	Tower of Cathedral 95 m (312 ft) Domstrasse Temporarily closed for repair
Henninger Tower (Henninger-Turm)	Henninger Tower 120 m (395 ft) Hainerweg 60–64 Panoramic revolving restaurant (45 minutes for each revolution) Open daily 10 a.m.–11.30 p.m.
Goethe Tower (Goethe-Turm)	Goethe Tower 43 m (141 ft) In Stadtwald above the Sachsenhäuser Berg, near the Goetheruhe play park Opening times as for play park: i.e. until sunset

Trade fairs

Information about all trade fairs and exhibitions in Frankfurt can be obtained from:

Messe- und Ausstellungsgesellschaft mbH,
Friedrich-Ebert-Anlage 57, tel. 75 75-1

See also Events, above

Travel agencies

There are more than 200 travel agencies and foreign tourist
offices in Frankfurt, with particular concentrations around the
Central Station (Kaiserstrasse) and Hauptwache (Goethestrasse, Steinweg, Zeil, Kornmarkt). Almost all of them are
listed in the "yellow pages" (gelbe Seiten) telephone directory
under the heading "Reisebüros". The travel agency departments of the large department stores in the Zeil deal mainly in
reasonably priced package tours; the agencies in the more
exclusive shopping streets handle more individual (and usually
more expensive) excursions.
The offices of the German National Tourist Office (Deutsche
Zentrale für Tourismus, DZT) are at Beethovenstrasse 69.

What are known in German as "incoming" travel agencies
(Incoming-Reisebüros) cater for the needs of visitors staying in
the city – accommodation, admission to trade fairs, conducted
tours with guide-interpreters, sightseeing programmes, etc.

"Incoming" travel agencies

American Express International Inc.,
Steinweg 5, tel. 21 05-02 26

DER Deutsches Reisebüro GmbH,
Eschersheimer Landstrasse 25, tel. 15 66-2 89
Branch in Central Station, tel. 23 09 11

Deutsche Touring GmbH (Europabus),
Am Römerhof 17, tel. 79 03-2 19

F.A.G. Flughafen Frankfurt/Main AG,
Incoming Division,
Airport, tel. 6 90-46 09/-46 90

Hapag Lloyd Reisebüro GmbH,
Kaiserstrasse 20, tel. 28 06 51

Wagons-Lits Reisebüro,
Kaiserstrasse 72, tel. 26 87-2 17

What's on in Frankfurt

Details of current events (theatres, concerts, exhibitions; trade
fairs, etc.) are given in the Press ("Frankfurter Allgemeine
Zeitung", "Frankfurter Rundschau").

Daily Press

This official publication (with town plan), produced in
collaboration with the Office of Tourism and the Frankfurt
Tourist Office, contains information on tourism and on cultural,
sporting and other events in the city. It appears fortnightly, and

"Frankfurter Wochenschau"

can be obtained free of charge from the Römer information bureau on the Römerberg (see Information).

The "Frankfurter Wochenschau" lists exhibitions, theatrical programmes, concerts, congresses and conferences, trade fairs and sporting events, as well as hotels (with number of beds, rates and amenities), restaurants, museums, cultural institutes and the main sights and other features of interest.

"Frankfurter Theaterzeitung"

A monthly publication, available from the Municipal Theatres (Städtische Bühnen: see Theatres), which gives full programme information, theatre news, etc.

"Frankfurter, Lebendige Stadt"

A quarterly journal concerned with cultural and economic matters and tourism.

Calendar of Events (Veranstaltungsnachweis)

Published by the Office of Tourism (Amt für Fremdenverkehr), tel. 2 12-58 73.

Youth hostels

In Frankfurt

Haus der Jugend,
Deutschherrnufer 12 (between the Upper and Lower Main Bridges),
tel. 61 90 58
500 beds in 65 dormitories.

In surrounding area

Hochtaunus-Jugendherberge Oberreifenberg
(also suitable for family holidays)
Fritz-Emmel-Jugendherberge,
Limesstrasse,
D-6384 Schmitten 3, tel. 0 60 82/24 40

Jugendherberge Bad Homburg,
DJH-Haus Saalburg,
Meiereiberg 1,
D-6380 Bad Homburg,
tel. 0 61 72/2 39 50

Jugendherberge Rüsselsheim,
Hauptmann-Scheuermann-Weg 6,
D-6090 Rüsselsheim,
tel. 0 61 42/4 23 46

Jugendherberge Darmstadt,
Am Grossen Woog, Landgraf-Georg-Strasse 119
D-6100 Darmstadt,
tel. 0 61 51/4 52 93

Information

Further information can be obtained from:

Deutsches Jugendherbergswerk,
Landesverband Hessen,
Stegstrasse 33,
D-6000 Frankfurt am Main 70,
tel. 62 10 33

Useful Telephone Numbers

Emergencies
    Police   7 55-1

Emergencies	
Police	7 55-1
Police (assault or traffic accident)	1 10
Police (central traffic accident service)	28 73 51
Fire, rescue service, first aid	1 12
Medical emergency service	79 20-2 00
Ambulance service	49 00 01
Chemists – out-of-hours service	11 50
Breakdown assistance:	
ACE	23 29 29
ADAC	74 30-6
AvD	6 66-16 66
Advice Centre for handicapped	2 12-34 07
Contact point for handicapped and chronic sick	53 02-2 57
Rescue helicopter	44 10 33

Information	
Tourist Information Office	23 10 55/23 22 18
Office of Tourism	2 12-36 77
Römertelefon	2 12-40 00/-41 00
Flight information	6 90-30 51
Train information	23 03 33/23 03 21

Motoring organisations	
ACE	23 51 58
ADAC	74 30-1
AvD	6 60-63 00
DTC	72 22 23

Lost property	
Municipal transport	13 68-22 58
Municipal Lost Property Office	75 00-24 03
Airport	6 90-24 13
Railways	2 65-58 31

Taxis	23 00 01/25 00 01

Telephone	
Information (calls within Germany)	1 18
Information (international calls)	0 01 18
International exchange	00 10

Telegrams	
In German	1 13
In any other language	11 13

Notes